All about God

All About God

MARY ROSE PEARSON

Tyndale House Publishers
Wheaton, Illinois

CONTENTS

Suggestions for Parents and Teachers

These days, perhaps more than at any other time, children need to be solidly grounded in the Word of God to survive in a world where it is denied, ridiculed, and ignored. They must know what the truth is and have a firm understanding of why they should believe it. Christian children need to know how to give an answer for the hope that is within them (1 Peter 3:15).

All about God is a perfect tool for introducing children to great doctrinal truths. Whether used for family devotions or in a classroom, these simple stories illustrate basic truths from God's Word through the everyday experiences of four children. As they learn about God, the Bible, angels, sin, salvation, Christian living, and other major Bible themes, the children you are teaching will learn, too.

After you have read each story aloud with clarity and enthusiasm, ask questions to see if the children were listening and understood the meaning. Follow this with a discussion of the truths contained in the story, using the suggested questions under "To discuss."

To help children apply the Bible, I've included a "To do" section. Many of these activities involve simple drawings, with a few added words, so that even the younger children may participate. Children may enjoy collecting their work in a loose-leaf notebook.

Encourage children to learn the memory verses. They will give the children a wealth of knowledge from God's Word. You can also delvelop children's Bible skills by helping them use their own Bibles to look up the verses.

May our Lord bless you as you endeavor to reach the children God

May our Lord bless you as you endeavor to reach the children God has placed in your life—whether at home, church, or school. It is the responsibility and privilege of those of us who have been taught to pass our knowledge on to the next generation (Psalm 71:17-18).

Mrs. Mary Rose Pearson

PART 1

God Is Real

KEY MEMORY VERSES

Psalm 19:1-3

The heavens declare the glory of God;
And the firmament shows His handiwork.
Day unto day utters speech,
And night unto night reveals knowledge.
There is no speech nor language
Where their voice is not heard.   *NKJV*

CHAPTER ONE

Romans 1:20
Since earliest times men have seen the earth and sky and all God made, and have known of his existence and great eternal power. So they will have no excuse [when they stand before God at Judgment Day]. TLB

Is There a Real God?

Joshua smiled as he hurried home from church. He could hardly wait for some of Mom's fried chicken! Then he met Mike. "You've been to church, haven't you?" asked Mike. "Why do you bother? There isn't any God, you know."

"Sure there's a God," said Joshua.

"Prove it," challenged Mike. "You can't see, hear, or touch him."

Joshua didn't know what to say. He did believe in God. But how could he prove that God is real? "I don't know what to tell you now, but I'm going to find out," he said.

That afternoon, at Grandpa's farm, Joshua said, "Grandpa, Mike said today that there isn't any God. I know he's wrong, but I couldn't prove it. How do you know God is real?"

Grandpa took Joshua out to the barn. Reaching into a bin, Grandpa picked out a kernel of corn. "Tomorrow I'm going to plant this seed," he said.

3

"Let's just imagine that it can talk. It says, 'I'm going to become a big stalk with long green leaves and many ears full of golden, juicy kernels of corn. Each kernel will be just like me.'

"'Why,' I would answer, 'you could never do that. Look at you—you're just one tiny, hard kernel. How are you going to change yourself like that?'

"'Oh,' says the kernel, 'I'll tell the sun to shine down and warm the earth and give me the light I need to grow. I'll ask the world to turn so I don't get too much sun. I'll make summer stay here long enough for me to finish my task. Of course, I'll call on the clouds to send rain. I'll choose minerals from the earth to help me. Then, with my power, I'll cause a little plant to burst out of my hard shell, push its way through the earth, and begin to grow on top of it.'"

Joshua laughed. "That would be a very silly little kernel, wouldn't it?" he said. "It has no power of its own to change itself into a big stalk of corn."

"Yet someday I expect it to become

a tall stalk with big green leaves and many ears full of golden, juicy kernels," Grandpa declared. "How can that be? I can't do anything but plant the seed and water it. The smartest scientist can't bring a plant out of this seed. And certainly this little kernel has no power to cause a plant to burst forth from this hard shell."

Joshua grinned. "Yeah," he said. "Without all those things, that kernel might as well be a yellow glass bead."

"Right," agreed Grandpa. "There is only one Source of all that power—God himself." Just then a hen cackled and left her nest. Grandpa picked up her egg, saying, "Only God can give that hen the ability to form this egg, which could either be your breakfast or a safe, warm home for a developing chick.

"Look all about you, Joshua. All that you see in nature is God's creation, plainly telling us, 'God's up there!'"

"Why didn't I think of that?" asked Joshua. "I'm gonna find some more ways to know God is real, too. When I tell them to Mike, I bet you then he'll believe in him!"

TO DISCUSS

Is there a God? How can you know for sure? What proofs did Grandpa give to Joshua that God exists? A person could make a yellow glass bead and plant it. Would it grow into a stalk of corn? What would be missing?

TO DO

Today take time to notice the things in nature that only God could have made. Write down a list of these on a piece of paper.

TO PRAY

Thank God for making our world. Ask him to help you see in nature many reasons to believe in him.

CHAPTER TWO

Job 38:8,11

Or who shut in the sea with doors, . . . [and] said, "This far you may come, but no farther, and here your proud waves must stop!" NKJV

Psalm 104:24

How many are your works,
  O Lord!
In wisdom you made them
  all;
the earth is full of your
  creatures. NIV

God's Footprints

Oh, I didn't know the ocean was so big!" exclaimed Sara, Joshua's cousin. "There's nothing like this in Kansas."

Joshua showed Sara how to build a sand castle. Soon after they finished it, the water began to creep close and nibble the sand away. "Look!" cried Sara. "The ocean's moving! It's washing away our castle. What's happening?"

"The tide's coming in," explained Joshua. "The water always comes in like this at high tide."

"Will it keep coming?" asked Sara. "Will we all drown?"

"It will stop soon," said Joshua. "You can count on it."

Sara started running. "Come on!" she yelled. "Let's get in the car, just to be sure. If it comes, we'll outrun it."

"Sara thinks the ocean will cover the whole land," Joshua told his dad.

7

"Do you know why its waters will never do that?" Dad asked.

"No," answered Joshua. "I just know they won't do it."

"The Bible tells us that God holds the ocean back," Dad explained. "He keeps everything in nature going. He causes the earth to turn, at just the right distance from the sun, too. Can you think of some more things he does?"

"He gives us food to eat and water to drink," Sara said.

"Yeah, and air to breathe," added Joshua. "If he wasn't in charge, we'd all die. Hey, that's another reason we know there's a God! You see, Sara, I want to show my friend Mike that God is real."

"Well, I'm glad God's in charge of the ocean," said Sara, "because I can't swim!"

"Wait for me," a voice called. It was Mike. "I knew I'd find you if I followed your footprints in the sand," he said.

"How did you know they were ours?" asked Joshua.

"Because you've got funny marks on the bottom of your sneakers, Josh. I always know your footprints," replied Mike.

"Mike, Joshua says you don't believe there's a God, because you can't see him," Joshua's dad said. "Did you know that we can see God's footprints on this earth?"

Mike's mouth fell open. "His footprints? Where are they? How do you know they're his, Mr. Kendrick?"

"He's left his footprints in nature," replied Mr. Kendrick.

"God made the ocean, the sand, the trees, the sun, and everything," explained Joshua. "They couldn't make themselves."

"We know God is real, because he's still taking care of the things he made—like keeping the ocean in its place and sending rain and giving us air to breathe," Mr. Kendrick said.

"Yeah, and the earth and the sun and the moon don't all bump together," added Sara. "God makes them stay put."

"We can see God's footprints all through history, too," added Mr. Kendrick. "He has often worked miracles to help people."

"Wow!" exclaimed Mike. "God's footprints! I never thought much about how our earth got here, or who takes care of it. Maybe I'd better learn more about God. Will you help me?"

Joshua grinned. That's just what he wanted to hear!

TO DISCUSS

Why don't the oceans flood the earth? Why doesn't the moon fall on us? What do you think would happen if the earth got closer to the sun than it is?

Or farther away? Can you think of some other ways God cares for his world? Could we live one minute without God? Is he real?

TO DO

On a piece of paper, draw a picture of yourself, standing between a mountain and the ocean. Place a sun and clouds in the sky. Explain to someone how God takes charge of each thing in your picture to keep you safe and well.

TO PRAY

Thank God that you are alive because he takes care of everything. Thank him for loving and caring for you.

CHAPTER THREE

John 20:31
But these things are written that you may believe that Jesus is the Christ, the Son of God, and that believing you may have life in His name.
NKJV

The Bible Tells about God

Joshua knocked at Mike's door. When Mike answered, he said, "Hi, Mike. Do you want to come over to my house and learn something about God? Mom has time to talk to us now."

Mike looked up from something he was reading. "Sure thing," he said. "I'd like to come."

"Hey, what have you got there?" Joshua asked.

"A letter from my grandpa," answered Mike. "I'll read it to you over at your house."

After he finished reading the letter, Mike said, "Isn't he the greatest grandpa in the whole world? He's kind and good, and he really loves me. I've never met my grandpa. He lives in Germany. But I know what he's like by reading his letters."

"Mike," said Mrs. Kendrick, Joshua's mother, "we've never seen God, either. But we have a way to know all about him." She held up her Bible. "Here it is—God's letters to us."

"That's the Bible, isn't it?" asked Mike. "Who wrote it?"

"I know," said Joshua. "God wrote it."

"Yes," agreed his mother. "God wrote sixty-six letters in the Bible to tell us all we need to know about him."

"What kind of pen and paper did he use?" Mike asked. "How did he get it down to earth?"

"God didn't write the words on paper himself," Joshua explained. "He told people what to write, and they wrote it down."

"Mike, when your grandpa's letters come, do you put them away, unopened?" Mrs. Kendrick asked.

"Oh no! I read Grandpa's letters over and over."

"And every time we read the Bible, we're reading God's letters over and over," Mrs. Kendrick told him. "That's how we get to know God better."

"Let's read some now, Mike," said Joshua, getting a Bible.

"Start reading with the book of John," his mom told them.

So Mike and Joshua headed for the porch swing to begin to learn more about God.

TO DISCUSS

Why do you think God wrote the Bible? What do you think God wants you to do with your Bible? Can you learn much about him without reading the Bible? How often should you read it? If you aren't doing so, will you try very hard to read his Book often?

TO DO

Make a Bible reading chart for this month. Make a square for each day, as in a calendar. Decide how many verses you'll read each day. Then, when you read them, place a star for that day on your chart. Perhaps, like Joshua and Mike, you would like to begin reading in John.

TO PRAY

Thank God for giving us his Book so we can learn about him. Ask him to help you remember to read it.

Hebrews 11:6
You can never please God without faith, without depending on him. Anyone who wants to come to God must believe that there is a God and that he rewards those who sincerely look for him. TLB

Answered Prayer Proves God Is Real

Mike burst into the Kendrick's house without knocking. "Mrs. Kendrick . . . Joshua," he called. "Where are you?"

Mrs. Kendrick and Joshua hurried to the door and found Mike excited and out of breath.

"What's wrong, Mike?" Mrs. Kendrick asked.

"My little sister, Kay, fell into our pool," Mike said. "Mom pulled her out, but she isn't breathing. I called 9-1-1."

Mrs. Kendrick and the two boys rushed to the Murphy's backyard, where Mrs. Murphy was trying to revive Kay. "Please pray, Mrs. Kendrick," Mike pleaded. "Ask God to keep Kay from dying."

As Mrs. Kendrick and Joshua prayed, the wail of sirens could be heard. Soon an ambulance and other emergency equipment arrived.

While the paramedics worked on Kay, Mrs. Kendrick held Mrs. Murphy in her arms. "We are praying for Kay," she told her.

"I've never thought much about God," Mrs. Murphy said. "But if there is a God, I sure need him now." In only a few moments after that, Kay coughed and began to breathe on her own. She was placed in the ambulance and rushed to the hospital. In two days she was home again, well and happy.

Mike came over to thank the Kendricks. "Mom says to thank you for praying," he said. "She says she's beginning to think about God. And I am, too," he added. "You told me some good reasons for knowing he's real, but when he answered your prayers, I was sure of it."

Mrs. Kendrick smiled. "Yes, Mike," she said, "answered prayers surely do prove that God lives. Some people

may say that Kay would have been OK anyway. We will never know for sure. But we do know that she got better almost as soon as we started praying. I have had many prayers answered. This makes God seem more real to me all the time. Would you boys like to work out a puzzle about prayer that I found?" she asked. "It is called, 'Who Hears Our Prayers?'"

The boys agreed and were soon busy with the puzzle.

TO DISCUSS

Can you think of a time God answered a prayer? Did this make God seem more real to you?

TO DO

Solve the puzzle "Who Hears Our Prayers?"

TO PRAY

Thank God for hearing your prayers. If you can think of any way God has answered a prayer lately, thank him for that, too.

Who Hears Our Prayers?

Unscramble the mixed up words and fill in the blanks. Look up the Scripture verse to find a word, if necessary. Then arrange the circled letters to form the answer to the question given. (The numbers over the circles tell whether the letters are in the first or second word.)

1. Call upon the Lord every (A) D (Y). (Psalm 88:9)

   ____ ____ ____ .

2. Search for God with all your E (R) (A) T (H). (Jeremiah 29:13)

   ____ ____ ____ ____ ____

3. Ask, and it shall be (V) I (N) (E) G to you. (Matthew 7:7)

   ____ ____ ____ ____ ____

4. Have (H) A (F) I (T). (Hebrews 11:6)

   ____ ____ ____ ____ ____

5. When you pray, (E) B (E) V I E (L). (Mark 11:24)

   ____ ____ ____ ____ ____

WHO HEARS AND ANSWERS OUR PRAYERS?

Our ____ ____ ____ ____ ____ ____ ____ ____

____ ____ ____ ____ ____ ____

Answer is on page 223.

CHAPTER FIVE

Colossians 1:15

[Jesus] is the image of the invisible God, the firstborn over all creation.

John 14:9

Jesus replied, "Don't you even yet know who I am, Philip, even after all this time I have been with you? Anyone who has seen me has seen the Father! So why are you asking to see him? TLB

When God Came to Earth

Hey, Mike, come over here," Joshua called to his friend. "I have a new game. My uncle sent it to me. It has blue and red pieces that fit on this—" Joshua stopped. "It would be much easier if I showed you. Wait here. I'll get it."

Joshua got his new game and the boys played it all afternoon. That evening Mike said to Mrs. Kendrick, "I do believe now that God is real and alive. I want to know more about him. But he's invisible. How can we know what he's really like?"

"How did you find out what Joshua's new game was really like?" asked Mrs. Kendrick. "Was it by hearing about it or seeing and playing the game itself?"

"Seeing and playing it!" Mike answered.

Mrs. Kendrick smiled. "And how do you suppose

19

people came to know what God the Father is really like?" she asked.

The boys looked puzzled. Then Joshua grinned. "I know," he said. "It was when God came to earth. You know, Mike, Jesus is God."

"Oh yeah, I've heard about him," answered Mike. "But I thought Jesus was a man."

"He was," said Joshua. "But he is

God, too. You see, God sent his Son down to earth to be born as a baby and grow up to be a man. He was God and man at the same time."

"That's right," said Mrs. Kendrick. "When Jesus was on earth, he was sinless and perfect. He loved everyone. He did many miracles and taught wonderful things. When we learn about Jesus, we know what God is like. Jesus said, 'Whoever sees me sees the Father.'"

Mrs. Kendrick held up a mirror to Mike's face. "What do you see, Mike?" she asked.

Mike grinned. "I see my ugly face," he answered.

"Is it really your face or the image of your face?"

Mike looked puzzled. "Oh, I get you," he said after a moment. "It's my image."

"Jesus was the image of God—an exact copy," Mrs. Kendrick said. "To know about him is to know what God is like."

Briefly tell the story of Jesus feeding the 5,000. (You can read it from John 6:5-14, if you'd like). Tell how you think this story shows these things about God:

     1. He is Creator.
     2. He loves people.
     3. He takes care of people.
     4. He likes to use people in his work.
     5. He can do anything he wants to do.

Write these sentences on a piece of paper, filling in the blanks:

The best way to know what God the Father is like is by knowing what _____ is like.

The best way to learn what Jesus is like is by reading and studying the _____ .

Thank your heavenly Father for sending his Son into the world to show us what he is like.

PART **2**

God's Book, the Bible

2 Timothy 3:16-17

All Scripture is inspired of God, and is profitable for doctrine, for reproof, for correction, for instruction in righteousness, that the man of God may be complete, thoroughly equipped for every good work. *NKJV*

CHAPTER SIX

Psalm 119:105
*Your word is a lamp to my feet
And a light to my path.* NKJV

God Used Holy Men to Write His Book

Mr. Kendrick pulled his car to the side of the road and stopped. "I think I've turned down the wrong road, boys," he said to Joshua and Mike. "Get out the map, Joshua. I need to look at it again."

"I left it home, Dad," Joshua said. "After you looked at it, you said you knew where to go."

Mr. Kendrick grinned sheepishly. "I thought I did, but now I'm lost," he said. The boys were on their way home from a baseball game. Although he stopped several times, Mr. Kendrick could find no one who knew how to get them home. "I'll have to phone home," he said

25

finally. "Mom can look at the map and tell us where to go." At last they got home, very late.

The next time the boys were talking with Joshua's mom, Joshua said, "I've been thinking about these lessons we're having. Why don't we have a Bible club?"

"That's a great idea," his mother said. "Maybe you can think of a name for your club. Any ideas?"

"How about calling ourselves 'Bible Explorers'?" said Mike.

Joshua and Mrs. Kendrick liked the name. "Well, Bible Explorers, I've been thinking about your adventure on the way home from the game. We all need a guide to show us where we should go in our lives, just as you needed a map to show you how to get home. Who knows all about you and the way you should take?"

"God," said Joshua. "And his guide book is the Bible."

"My uncle says the Bible is the same as other books," said Mike. "How do you know God wrote it?"

"God said he wrote it, didn't he, Mom?" asked Joshua.

"Yes, he did," said Mrs. Kendrick. "Joshua, help Mike find 2 Timothy 3:16. How much of the Bible was inspired by God, Mike?"

Mike read the verse. "It says all Scripture was inspired by God," he replied.

"Mike, if God said he wrote the whole thing, then he did," Joshua said. "God always tells the truth."

"God only wrote a very small part of the Bible with his own fingers," Mrs. Kendrick said. "Joshua, tell Mike what that was."

"It was the Ten Commandments," Joshua said. "He wrote them on two tablets of stone and gave them to Moses."

"All the rest of the Bible was written by people that loved God," Mrs. Kendrick said. "There were about forty in all."

"How do you know they didn't make mistakes?" Mike asked.

"God's Holy Spirit put into their minds what to say," Mrs. Kendrick said. "He guided them to write his messages and carefully watched so there were no mistakes. It took around sixteen hundred years to complete the Bible, yet it's all true."

"How did God tell them what to say?" Mike wanted to know.

"He talked with some men in person," answered Mrs. Kendrick. "Others had dreams or visions. Some wrote things that they themselves had seen and heard. As they all wrote, God the Holy Spirit was helping them."

"I'm going to ask my folks to buy me a Bible," said Mike. "I'll read it every day to learn what God wants me to know."

TO DISCUSS

What are some areas that the Bible can help guide you? Why can you trust the Bible to be accurate?

TO DO

Copy Psalm 119:160 on a piece of paper. Make a wall hanging for your room. Ask for an old road map and cut out a section, about eight-by-ten inches. Glue this to cardboard. Print on the map, "The Bible is God's road map for my life."

TO PRAY

Ask God to help you learn his Word well enough so that you can use it as a guide for your life.

CHAPTER SEVEN

Matthew 24:35
Heaven and earth will disappear, but my words remain forever. TLB

Satan Can't Destroy the Bible

Do you know what happened at school today, Mrs. Kendrick?" Mike asked. "I told my friend that I believe God is real and the Bible is true. He told me that his dad says the Bible is a pack of lies and should be destroyed. Why would anyone want to get rid of the Bible?"

"Satan hates the Bible," said Mrs. Kendrick. "He has tried for many years to destroy it from the face of the earth. But God has never allowed all the copies to be destroyed. The fact that Satan can't destroy the Bible is one proof that it is truly from God."

"Mom, tell Mike the story from the Bible about the time a king burned up some of God's Word," said Joshua.

"That was King Jehoiakim," said Mrs. Kendrick.

29

"God told Jeremiah to write a message to the people, saying that they must quit sinning, or God would punish them. When the king listened to some of the message, he became very angry. He grabbed the scroll, cut it with his knife, and burned it up."

"Was that part of the Bible? Is some of God's Word missing, then?" asked Mike.

"Yes, it was part of the Bible," said Mrs. Kendrick. "But it is not missing

because God told Jeremiah to write the words again. They are here today, in the book of Jeremiah.

"Satan even tries to destroy the Bible today," Mrs. Kendrick continued. "There are still countries where people are thrown in prison or killed for owning a Bible. Many brave people have risked their lives to help those people learn about God. I'm sure that makes Satan very angry. But God is stronger than Satan, and God wants those people to learn about how much he loves them."

"I sure am glad God is stronger than Satan," Mike said. "And I'm glad he has protected his Word so that we can read it, too!"

TO DISCUSS

Do you know anybody who shows disrespect for the Bible? Are there times when you do not respect the Bible? Do you ever throw your Bible down or carelessly tear its pages? Do you talk or write notes to friends when it is being read? How can you show respect for the Bible?

TO DO

On the inside of your Bible, neatly print these words: God gave me this Book. I will use it carefully.

TO PRAY

Thank God for giving you his Word. Promise him that you will take good care of your Bible. Ask him to help you love and respect it always.

CHAPTER EIGHT

Galatians 1:11-12

I want you to know, brothers, that the gospel I preached is not something that man made up. I did not receive it from any man, nor was I taught it; rather, I received it by revelation from Jesus Christ. NIV

Only God Could Write the Bible's Message

It happened in an instant. As Joshua and Mike were peacefully walking down the sidewalk, two men burst through a nearby doorway, waving guns. As the men jumped into a car and sped away, a man ran out of the store, yelling, "They stole my money. Quick! Get their license plate number."

Soon the police arrived. Joshua and Mike had been the only witnesses, except for the store owner. "I saw the last three numbers on the license plate," said Mike. "They were 803."

"No, they weren't," said Joshua. "They were 388."

There were other things that the boys disagreed on. The store owner wasn't quite sure about some details, either.

When the boys told Mrs. Kendrick about the robbery, she was very surprised. "I'm glad you're both OK. You must have been very frightened."

"We're OK, Mom," said Joshua. "I just wish we could have gotten all the facts straight."

"Each person was probably right about some details and wrong about some others. But that is not unusual," said Mrs. Kendrick. "You were suddenly startled and very excited."

"Yeah," said Mike. "The policeman said that it's hard to notice every detail. He was glad there were at least three witnesses."

Mrs. Kendrick paused. "You know, the Bible had many witnesses. Do you know how many people God used to write it?"

"About forty different people," answered Mike.

"And over how long a period was the Bible written?"

"It took about sixteen hundred years," said Joshua.

"Here then is one more proof that God wrote the Bible," Mrs. Kendrick went on. "You see, even good people make mistakes or see things differently, just as you did at the robbery. Many of the forty Bible writers never knew each other. Some wrote far apart in time. Yet their writings fit together like a puzzle.

"The sixty-six books of the Bible make up one Book. It is complete and whole," Mrs. Kendrick went on. "There is one main theme, the gospel, and one central person, the Lord Jesus Christ."

"I've been reading my new Bible," said Mike. "I feel like it's talking to me, even though it was written so long ago."

Mrs. Kendrick nodded. "That's another proof that God wrote it," she said. "The Bible speaks to all persons of every age and race. It is for us, as well as for people who lived long ago. Its words live. They tell us how to be saved and how to live the Christian life. Who could write such a message?"

"Only God," replied Joshua. "Nobody else."

TO DISCUSS

What do you think would happen if two men tried to write one book on a subject without ever discussing it together? What if forty men tried to do it? Forty men did write one Book. What was it? Why aren't there mistakes in the Bible?

TO DO

If you know the song "The B-I-B-L-E," go ahead and sing it. On a piece of paper, draw an open Bible. Beneath it write, "The Bible is God's book."

TO PRAY

Thank the Lord for his wonderful Word, which only he could write. Thank him that even children can understand it.

CHAPTER NINE

Isaiah 40:22
It is God who sits above the circle of the earth. (The people below must seem to him like grasshoppers!) He is the one who stretches out the heavens like a curtain and makes his tent from them. TLB

John 17:17
. . . Your word is truth. NKJV

The Bible Is Right about Science and History

Wow! Isn't this exciting, Mike?" asked Joshua. "We're going to see the rocket take off any minute now."

"Yeah, I can hardly wait," said Mike. Standing by the river, across from Cape Canaveral, the boys and Joshua's parents looked toward the east. Suddenly there was a huge roar and a rumble that shook the earth. Then, with clouds of smoke and flame, the rocket sailed into the sky. What a sight!

Later on, as the boys watched TV at home, they saw pictures of the earth which the astronauts were sending back. "It looks like a great, big ball," said

Mike. "The people who lived long ago would sure be surprised to see that, because they thought the earth was flat."

"If they had read and believed this, they would have known better," Mr. Kendrick said, handing Mike a Bible. "Here, read the first part of Isaiah 40:22."

"Why, it says that God sits upon the circle of the earth," said Mike. "How did Isaiah know the earth was a circle?"

"Because God told him what to write," said Joshua. "Of course God knows the earth is round, because he made it."

"Right," said Mrs. Kendrick. "Boys, we've been talking about proofs that the Bible is true. Here is another one: the Bible is right about science. There is no difference between proven scientific facts and what the Bible says."

"My teacher says the Bible is wrong in what it says about creation," said Mike. "He believes in evolution."

"But evolution is just a theory, not proven facts," said Mr. Kendrick. "A person who thinks he's found a scientific mistake in the Bible doesn't really understand what the Bible says."

"Or else he hasn't learned all the facts yet," added Mrs. Kendrick. "For instance, God told us over three thousand years ago, in Job 38:7, that the 'morning stars sing together.' But only recently have scientists with their strong instruments begun to hear sounds coming from stars."

"Is the Bible right about history, too?" asked Mike.

"Yes, it is," answered Mr. Kendrick. "Here's one example: the Bible gives the names of some kings who lived long ago, and the people who deny the Bible used to say those kings never lived. Now, through digging in the earth and by studying old books, we know that those kings did live—and in the very places where the Bible says they did."

"Hey, I know how that can be," said Joshua. "God was there when everything happened. Of course he knew all about it."

TO DISCUSS

Who was present when the world was created? Who should know more about this earth—people who live in it, or the one who made it? The Bible wasn't written to teach us scientific facts, but when these facts are mentioned in the Bible they are always correct.

TO DO

Solve the puzzle "The Bible Said It Long Ago."

TO PRAY

Thank God that we can trust what the Bible says about science and history.

The Bible Said It Long Ago

Circle the word in each circle that does not belong. Print the circled words in the blanks to find what Isaiah said long ago about the shape of the earth. He said that God sits on his throne _____ _____ _____ _____ _____ _____.

cat	man	circle	yellow	frog	laugh
dog	the	boy	blue	snake	earth
above	woman	girl	of	the	cry

Answer is on page 224.

Romans 1:16

For I am not ashamed of this Good News about Christ. It is God's powerful method of bringing all who believe it to heaven. This message was preached first to the Jews alone, but now everyone is invited to come to God in this same way. TLB

The Bible Is God's Dynamite

It's going to blow any minute, boys," said Mr. Kendrick. "Watch that building." Suddenly, with a *POOF,* the bricks of the huge building tumbled down like toy building blocks, each one falling right where the building had stood.

"I can't believe it," said Mike. "Why didn't the bricks fall down all over this block?"

"Because the men who prepared the building for demolition knew how much dynamite to use and where to place it," answered Mr. Kendrick. "Now, would you like to hear about God's dynamite?"

"God's dynamite?" asked Joshua. "What's that?"

"The gospel is God's message about the Lord Jesus, who died on the cross for our sins and rose again," Mr. Kendrick answered. "A verse in the Bible, Romans 1:16, says that the gospel is the power of God. Another way to say that is, 'The gospel is the dynamite of God.'

"Listen to this story. It will show you how the Bible is God's dynamite. It's about a boy in high school who drank too much. In college he became an alcoholic and did many things that were not pleasing to God. At last he was kicked out of school. Then he heard the gospel message from the Bible. He believed it and asked Jesus to save him. His life was completely changed. He didn't want to do things that displeased God anymore. He graduated from college with honors. Boys, I was that young man."

"I've heard that story before," Joshua told Mike. "It's hard to believe Dad was ever that bad."

"I'm not proud of it," said his dad. "But God changed me. The gospel message is the power, or dynamite, of God. When I believed it and received Jesus as my Savior, God blew to pieces all the awful sins of my old life. Then he gave me a new life, just as they'll build a beautiful new building here.

"One of the best ways to know that the Bible is true is to see how people's lives are changed when they believe its message about sin and trust Jesus to save them."

"I'm glad you let God's dynamite work on you," said Joshua.

"I know you've let it work on you, too, Josh," Mike said. "You're different from my other friends. I guess that's why I like to be around you so much."

"Thanks, Mike," Joshua said.

To himself he thought, Mike looks real serious. I wonder if he's thinking that he needs his life changed, too. I sure hope he is!

TO DISCUSS

Many books tell you about ways in which you can change your life or do differently. But do the authors of those books have the power to make someone a new, different person? Can they forgive that person's sins? The Author of only one book can do that. Who is he? What book did he write?

TO DO

Begin to memorize these verses, so that you can tell the good news about Jesus to others: Romans 3:23 (all have sinned), Romans 5:8 (Jesus died for sinners), John 3:16 and Acts 16:31 (believe in Jesus as your Savior), and Romans 10:13 (whoever believes will be saved).

TO PRAY

Thank God for giving us the gospel message in the Bible. If you have not asked Jesus to forgive your sins and make you a new person, would you like to ask him now?

PART 3

What God Is Like

1 Timothy 1:17

Now to the King eternal, immortal, invisible, to God only wise, be honor and glory forever and ever. Amen.   *NKJV*

CHAPTER ELEVEN

Who Is God?

John 4:24

God is spirit, and his worshipers must worship him in spirit and in truth. NIV

Dark clouds raced across the sky, a few spatters of rain fell, and a gust of wind almost knocked Joshua and Mike off their bikes as they rode along. "Let's head for my house!" yelled Joshua. "A storm's coming!"

The boys got inside just as the storm broke. "How about some hot chocolate?" asked Mrs. Kendrick. "Then the Bible Explorers Club can meet."

"Good idea!" Joshua said.

As the boys finished their hot chocolate, Mike asked Mrs. Kendrick, "What does God look like? Does he have eyes and ears like ours? And hands and feet?"

"John 1:18 says that no one has seen God at any time," answered Mrs. Kendrick. "The Bible tells us that God is a spirit, which means he doesn't have a body. But it speaks of his eyes, ears, hands, and feet, though."

"I learned a verse that says, 'The eyes of the Lord are in every place, beholding the evil and the good,'" said Joshua.

His mom nodded. "That means God sees everything everywhere all at once. We can't

47

understand about seeing without thinking of eyes, so God uses the term *eyes*. It doesn't mean that he has eyes like ours, but that he sees. In the same way, the Bible uses other body parts to explain about God."

"How does God seem real to you, when he's just a spirit?" asked Mike.

"The same way the wind seemed real to you boys just now," answered Mrs. Kendrick. "You didn't see it, but you surely knew it was there. God is not imaginary, like a ghost. He's a living person, who knows, sees, hears, and loves. He can do anything he wants to. Those of us who have received Jesus as Savior know he's real because he lives inside us."

"I know he's real," said Joshua. "I talked to him this morning."

Mike was silent for a moment. Then he said, "Well, God's been talking to me down inside—you know, about getting saved. Would you help me ask Jesus to save me?"

And soon, although the storm raged outside the house, there was peace inside Mike's heart. He didn't see God, but he knew for sure that he is real.

TO DISCUSS

Does God have a body, such as we have? Why does the Bible talk about his eyes, ears, arms, hands, feet, and so on? How can you know God is real? Who will see God someday?

TO DO

Down the side of a piece of paper, draw an eye, an ear, a hand, and a foot. Alongside each drawing, write something that God does. For instance, next to your drawing of an eye, you might write, "God watches over me." At the bottom, write, "God is a person."

TO PRAY

Thank God that he sees you, hears you, takes care of you, and walks beside you in life. Ask him to help you understand more and more what he is like.

CHAPTER TWELVE

Psalm 90:1-2
*Lord, through all generations
you have been our home!
Before the mountains were
    created,
before the earth was formed,
you are God without
beginning or end.* TLB

Jeremiah 23:24
*"Can anyone hide himself in
    secret places,
So I shall not see him?" says
    the Lord;
Do I not fill heaven and
    earth?" says the Lord.* NKJV

Where Is God? How Long Has He Lived?

Joshua and Mike were playing in a storage shed in back of Mike's house. Suddenly the wind blew the door shut. *BANG!* Mike looked through his pockets for the key. "Uh-oh!" he exclaimed. "That door has to open with a key, and I can't find mine. Help me look for it."

The boys searched carefully throughout the shed. "I must have dropped it outside," said Mike. "Now what are we going to do? It will be forever till our folks find us, because they don't know we're here."

The boys banged on the door and yelled loudly.

But no one answered. The shed was hot and stuffy, and soon it was totally dark. "I'm getting scared, Josh," said Mike. "I don't like to be here in the dark all by ourselves."

"But we're not by ourselves," Joshua said. "God is here."

"He's HERE? That can't be," said Mike. "God's in heaven."

"Sure, but he's here, too," replied

Joshua. "The Bible says God is so big that he's everywhere at once."

"If I could see him, I wouldn't be so scared," said Mike.

"You don't have to see him, " Joshua said. "Let's ask him right now to take care of us and send someone to help us."

Soon after they prayed, a voice called, "Mike, are you in there?"

"That's my dad!" exclaimed Mike. "God IS here, and he sent help. I'm sure glad he's everywhere at once."

The next day Mike said to Mrs. Kendrick, "I still have a lot to learn about God. Yesterday, when we were locked in the shed, Joshua told me that God is everywhere—even in a dark shed."

"Yes, sometimes we think God is far away, up in heaven, especially when we feel lonely or afraid," answered Mrs. Kendrick. "It's great to know he's always with us."

"Tell me some more about God," said Mike. "Where did he come from? Did he have parents? Was he born in heaven?"

"No, God was never born, and no

one made him. He's always been alive," Mrs. Kendrick answered.

"Whew! That sort of scrambles my mind," said Mike. "I can't imagine someone with no beginning."

"Think way back to when there wasn't an earth or the sun or the moon," said Joshua. "God was living then. No matter how far you go back in your mind, God was there. It sure does scramble your mind. I always feel like there ought to be a starting point somewhere."

"Will God ever die?" asked Mike.

"Oh no," said Mrs. Kendrick. "The Bible calls him 'the everlasting God.' He is forever."

"I've been so happy since Jesus came into my heart," said Mike. "I'm glad he'll go on and on and never stop. That's hard to understand, too. But I believe it."

TO DISCUSS

How can it help you to know that God is with you when you are lonesome . . . afraid . . . lost . . . tempted to sin? Where were you ten years before you were born? Who was living a trillion years before you were born? Only God has no beginning or ending. He says so in the Bible.

TO DO

1. On a piece of paper, carefully draw around a round object, like a saucer. Leave no marks where you begin or end. Inside the circle, print "God." Underneath the circle, print, "From everlasting to everlasting."

2. Make a sign to hang on your wall. Glue a piece of construction paper to cardboard. Decorate the edges with crayons or felt markers. Inside, print, "Do not fear, for I am with you." (Read Isaiah 41:10.)

TO PRAY

Thank the Lord that you can always count on him to be with you.

CHAPTER THIRTEEN

Job 42:2

Then Job replied to God: "I know that you can do anything and that no one can stop you." TLB

Matthew 19:26

Jesus looked at them and said, "With man this is impossible, but with God all things are possible." NIV

Psalm 147:5

Great is our Lord, and mighty in power; His understanding is infinite. NKJV

What Can God Do? How Much Does He Know?

Look, down there on the corner, Mike," said Joshua. "That looks like trouble. I think that big guy is trying to take Tim's bike away from him."

"Let's go see if we can help Tim," said Mike. Quickly, the boys headed for the corner. The closer they got, the more they realized that the big boy was very big indeed. He had one hand on Tim's arm and the other on his bike.

"Hey! Let go of him!" screamed Joshua, sounding braver than he felt. He prayed silently to God for help.

"Says who?" snarled the bully, before he even turned to see who it was.

"We do—Mike and me," answered Joshua.

The bully let go of the bike and pushed Tim to the ground. Then he stepped toward Joshua. Just then a police car rounded the corner and slowly started down the street. When the bully saw it, he backed away from Joshua and ran down the street.

"Wow, that was scary!" said Tim. "Thanks, guys, for coming to help me."

"Your real help came from God," Joshua told him. "I prayed for his help, and he sent that police car along, just in time."

Later, at Bible Explorers Club, Mike said, "I felt so small and helpless when that bully threatened us. I forgot that I could call on God for his help. I'm glad Josh remembered."

"God is more powerful than any person," said Mrs. Kendrick. "He can do anything he wants to do.

"Another great thing about God," said Mrs. Kendrick, "is that he knows all things. He saw you boys when you felt alone and helpless as you stood up to that bully. Even beforehand, he knew what was going to happen, and he sent the police car into our neighborhood."

"Yeah, it came just at the right time," said Mike. "I'm finding out lots of good things about God."

TO DISCUSS

Look up Judges 14:5-6. Who was the strongest man who ever lived? From whom did he get his strength? When did Samson lose his strength? Suppose there were ten thousand giants on one side, ready to fight, and one person—God—on the other side. Whose side would you want to be on?

TO DO

Solve the puzzle "What Does God Know?" First, look up each verse and fill in the blanks for statements 1 to 9. Write these words again under number 10. Read John 16:30. What does God know?

TO PRAY

God likes to help us with our problems. If you need God's help with anything right now, ask him.

What Does God Know?

1. *Psalm 147:4*   The names of all the _____ .
2. *John 21:16*   If you _____ him.
3. *Acts 5:4*   If someone _____ to him.
4. *Acts 15:8*   Your _____ .
5. *Psalm 139:2*   Your _____ .
6. *Matthew 10:30* The number of _____ you have.
7. *Matthew 6:8*   What you _____ .
8. *Proverbs 15:3* The wicked and the _____ .
9. *Psalm 139:3*   All your _____ .

10.   John 16:30

1. ____ ____ ____ ____ ____

2. ____ ____ ____ ____

3. ____ ____ ____

4. ____ ____ ____ ____ ____

5. ____ ____ ____ ____ ____ ____

6. ____ ____ ____ ____

7. ____ ____ ____ ____

8. ____ ____ ____ ____

9. ____ ____ ____ ____

Answer is on page 225.

CHAPTER FOURTEEN

1 Peter 2

But just as he who called you is holy, so be holy in all you do; for it is written: "Be holy as I am holy." NIV

Malachi 3:6

For I am the Lord, I do not change. . ." NKJV

God Is Holy and Never Changes

Thanks for taking us on this hike, Dad," said Joshua. "I'm glad you're our Sunday school teacher. You let us do lots of fun things."

"I hope you'll still think it's fun if the girls and your mom beat us to the picnic area," said his dad. "They chose the other path, but I'm sure this one will get us there faster." After a turn in the path, he exclaimed, "Oh no! Our path ends in a barnyard. We'll have to go back. Let's hurry!"

When they finally came huffing and puffing up to the picnic area, the girls chanted, "The girls beat the boys! Yaah, yaah!"

"It's not the boys' fault," said Mrs. Kendrick. "They just followed the wrong leader."

After their picnic, Mr. Kendrick said, "I'll admit I led the boys astray today. Kids, many times in life

59

you will need to choose which way you should go. Perhaps someone will say, 'Follow me. I'll show you the right way.' Or maybe you'll decide to go along with the crowd and do what they are doing.

"There is no human being that doesn't make mistakes sometimes. Even Christians who love the Lord very much are not perfect. All of us

make mistakes. The only one you can always safely follow is the Lord. He'll never lead you down the wrong path. Why?"

"Because he always does right," Joshua said. "He's holy."

"That's right," said Mr. Kendrick. "That means God is separate from sin."

"Another great thing about God is that he never changes," added Mrs. Kendrick. "We can always count on him to be the same. A change must be for the better or the worse. Could God be better than he is?"

"Of course not," said Joshua. "He's already perfect. And, of course, he can't change for the worse."

"Read your Bible and pray to learn what God wants you to do," said Mr. Kendrick. "Obey him always, and he'll never let you down or disappoint you."

"And be sure your leader on a hike knows where he's going," said Mrs. Kendrick, with a wink at the girls.

TO DISCUSS

The Bible says we are to follow in Jesus' steps. What do you think that means? Would Jesus' steps ever lead you to steal, lie, disobey your parents, or do anything wrong? Read 1 Peter 1:16. Why are we to be separate from sin?

TO DO

Divide a piece of paper into two columns. Label one of them, "Things That Jesus' Steps Will Not Lead Me to Do." Label the other, "Things That Jesus' Steps Will Lead Me to Do." Write as many things in each column as you can. On another page, draw a crooked line. Under it print, "What people are like." Using a ruler, make a straight line. Under it print, "What God is like." At the bottom print, "God is holy. He never changes."

TO PRAY

Thank the Lord that he is holy and never changes. Ask him to help you follow in Jesus' steps always.

CHAPTER FIFTEEN

Deuteronomy 32:36
*For the Lord will judge His
   people
And have compassion on His
   servants.* NKJV

Romans 5:8
*But God demonstrates His
own love toward us, in that
while we were yet sinners,
Christ died for us.* NKJV

God Is Fair and Right; He Is Love

Joshua, it's just not fair. I got punished for something I didn't do," Mike complained to his friend.

"What happened?" asked Joshua.

"Chuck was playing with my ball, and he accidentally smashed Mr. Hill's window," Mike explained. "Chuck told Mr. Hill I did it. Mr. Hill believed Chuck, because he saw my initials on the ball. Mr. Hill told my dad, and I got grounded all day. That's why I didn't come to play with you."

The next day, Mike told Mrs. Kendrick about his unfair punishment. "People aren't perfect judges of right and wrong, are they?" asked Mrs. Kendrick. "There is one, though, who is fair at all times. The Bible tells us that God is just and righteous. That is, he is fair and right in dealing with everyone. What does Romans 3:23 say that all people have done?"

"We have sinned," Mike answered.

"If God is absolutely fair and right, can he simply overlook sin as unimportant?" Mrs. Kendrick asked.

Mike shook his head. "Nope," he answered. "God has to punish sin, if he's fair and right."

"Yes, he must judge it," said Mrs. Kendrick. "So he has ruled that sinners must be punished in hell forever."

"But not if they believe in Jesus," said Joshua.

"Isn't that wonderful?" asked Mrs. Kendrick, with a smile. "God loves us so much that he sent his Son to take our punishment by dying on the cross. Then he says we may escape punishment by trusting Jesus to forgive our sins. God's love is so great that we can't simply say that he loves. He is love.

"Before God made the earth, he knew we'd all sin," Mrs. Kendrick continued. "Still, he created Adam and Eve and started the human race. But, before he did, he planned that

his own Son would come and take the punishment for sin."

"Wow!" exclaimed Mike. "He knew we'd sin, but he made us, anyway. That's great!"

"Yes," said Mrs. Kendrick, "and, as soon as we accept Jesus as Savior, God makes us his children. Joshua, can you name some ways God has shown his love to you since you were saved?"

"Oh, there are just lots of ways," answered Joshua. "He takes care of me and answers my prayers and helps me every day."

"Not a day goes by that we can't all find a thousand ways to know that God loves us," said Mrs. Kendrick. "And that's how we know that he will always treat us fair and right."

TO DISCUSS

What are some special things God has done for you because of his love for you? Is there anything you could do that would make God quit loving you? Even if you disobey God, and he disciplines you in some way, he never stops loving you. If God allows bad things to happen in your life, what should you remember?

TO DO

Write the following verse references down the side of a piece of paper. Read each verse and write beside it who God loves: John 3:35, John 3:16, Ephesians 2:4-5, John 16:27, Hosea 11:1. At the bottom of your page, write, "Jesus loves me."

TO PRAY

Thank God for his great love. Ask him to help you show your love for him today.

PART 4

One in Three

KEY MEMORY VERSE

Isaiah 45:22

Look to Me, and be saved,
All you ends of the earth!
For I am God, and there is no other.   *NKJV*

CHAPTER SIXTEEN

2 Corinthians 13:14
May the grace of the Lord Jesus Christ, and the love of God, and the fellowship of the Holy Spirit be with you all. NIV

How Many Gods Are There?

I have good news," Joshua's mom told him one day. "Your cousin Sara and her folks are moving here from Kansas. Uncle Steve and Aunt Faye will drive the moving van here. Sara is flying in soon and will stay with us until they arrive."

"Hey, that's great!" said Joshua. "I like Sara. She's pretty cool—for a girl."

A week later, Joshua and his mom picked up Sara at the airport. "I was scared because I've never flown before," Sara said. "I asked Daddy how that big plane could stay in the air. He said he really doesn't understand how, but he's flown many times, and the planes always stayed in the air. He said, 'You just get on the plane and trust it to take you to Aunt Betty's.' So I did, and here I am!"

That afternoon the Bible Explorers met with

Mrs. Kendrick and Sara joined them. "Our next theme is 'The One God Is Three Persons.' It isn't an easy subject for us to understand, but we know it's true."

"Well, I sure don't understand how three can be one," said Sara. "How can we believe in something we can't understand?"

"Sara, you didn't understand how your airplane could stay in the air," said her aunt. "But you believed your father when he said it would fly you safely, so you got on the plane and enjoyed the trip, didn't you?

"We don't need to understand that one God is three persons," explained Mrs. Kendrick. "The Bible says it, so we believe it. In Deuteronomy 6:4 God says, 'The Lord our God is one

Lord.' Other Scriptures tell us of three different persons of the Godhead. Who are they?"

"I know," answered Joshua. "They are the Father, the Son, and the Holy Spirit?"

"That's right," replied his mom. "All three persons are equal, and they are the same God. They agree about everything perfectly. They are different only in the works they do. When we get to heaven, we'll understand better about God."

"Maybe now we can't understand because we don't know God's mathematics," suggested Mike.

TO DISCUSS

Read Mark 1:9-11. When Jesus was baptized, the three persons of the Godhead were present. What was the Son doing? In what form did the Holy Spirit come down? What did the Father do?

TO DO

All three persons of the Godhead had something to do with your salvation. Look up these verses and fill the blanks to see what each did:
1. The Father_____ the Son to be the Savior (I John 4:14).
2. The Son_____for your sins and_____again (I Corinthians 15:3-4).
3. The Holy Spirit causes you to be_____ into God's family (John 3:5-6).

TO PRAY

Thank God that, although you can't understand all about him, you can know about him from the Bible.

CHAPTER SEVENTEEN

Galatians 3:26
For in Christ Jesus you are all children of God through faith.
NRSV

What Is God the Father Like?

Sara rushed into the next Bible Explorers meeting a few minutes late and said in an excited voice, "Guess what? There is a girl just my age who lives in the house next to where I'm going to live. Her name is Jodie. She's nice. Now I'll have someone to play with."

"Jodie's that adopted girl," said Mike. "We know her."

"She's adopted?" asked Sara, surprised. "Well, she sure is proud of her parents. She says they're great."

"She should be proud of them," said Mrs. Kendrick. "Jodie was a very unhappy girl when they took her in. Her folks had abandoned her. A couple of years ago, someone found Jodie beside the road, dirty and hungry, and with bruise marks all over her. She said her folks told her they didn't want her anymore, and they just dumped her beside the road. Now the Taylors have adopted her and are giving her a good home."

"Yeah, Jodie told me she used to be scared and unhappy all the time. Now she's real happy in her new home," Joshua said.

"Children," said Mrs. Kendrick, "did you know that you have all been adopted, too?"

Joshua's mouth flew open. "Adopted? Me?" he said.

Mrs. Kendrick smiled. "Oh, you're my own flesh-and-blood son," she said. "But I'm talking about your spiritual life. You see, when you were born into this world, you were not

God's child. You were born a sinner. But when you trusted Jesus as your Savior, you were born into God's family. He became your heavenly Father."

"I'm real glad God adopted me," said Mike. "I sure am happy to be his child."

"There are some special works that God the Father does for us," said Mrs. Kendrick. "We will look up some verses to find out about a few of them. Aren't you glad we have such a wonderful heavenly Father?"

TO DISCUSS

Look up the verses that Mrs. Kendrick gave the children and discover what God the Father does for his children:
1. John 1:12
2. John 10:27-29
3. Matthew 6:32 and Philippians 4:19
4. Matthew 6:6
5. Hebrews 12:6-7

TO DO

If you are God's child, make your own "new birth" certificate. Decorate the edges of a piece of paper with crayons or paints. At the top print, "New Birth Certificate." Underneath write, "I, [your full name], was made a child of God on [put down the date, if you know it; if not, put today's date] at [put down the place] when I received Jesus as my Savior." At the bottom print the words of John 1:12.

TO PRAY

If you are saved, thank God that he is your heavenly Father. If you aren't saved, would you like to ask him to make you his child now?

CHAPTER EIGHTEEN

God the Son

1 John 4:9,15

This is how God showed his love among us: He sent his one and only Son into the world that we might live through him. . . . If anyone acknowledges that Jesus is the Son of God, God lives in him and he in God. NIV

Aunt Betty, Jodie doesn't know anything about Jesus," said Sara. "When I talked about him, she asked me who he is. She's never heard of him."

"And I'm sure her new parents haven't told her about him, either," said Mrs. Kendrick. "The Taylors are good, kind people, but they aren't Christians."

"Well, Jodie wants to learn about Jesus," said Sara. "Could she come to our Bible Explorers Club?"

Mrs. Kendrick smiled. "Of course she may," she replied.

At the next meeting, Jodie was there. "Sara says Jesus is somebody very important," she said. "Please tell me about him."

"We'd love to," Mrs. Kendrick said. "First of all, Mike, will you tell Jodie who made our world and takes care of it?"

"God does," said Mike. "We can't see him, but he's real. He lives in heaven. He has lived forever and ever, and he'll never die."

"God can do anything he wants to do," added Sara. "He knows everything, too, like when we do wrong. But he loves us, and he does good things for us. And, oh yes, he never sins."

"How do you know all this?" Jodie asked.

"There are many ways to know about God," answered Mrs. Kendrick. "But the best way is by reading this special Book which he wrote—the Bible. It tells us that God is in three persons: the Father, the Son, and the Holy Spirit.

"Long, long ago, before there was an earth, God the Son lived in heaven with his Father. He had always been there. Beautiful angels worshiped him and served him, for he was the King of Glory. Finally, he created this earth. He made plants, birds, fish, and animals. Then he made people.

"The first two people were Adam and Eve," Mrs. Kendrick continued. "They were pure and good when God made them, but they disobeyed him and became sinners. God must always punish sin. But, because he loves people so much, he promised Adam and Eve he would send a Savior to take the punishment for sin.

"A long time went by. God sent many prophets to tell the people that a Savior would come into the world. The people waited and wondered when that would be. Some gave up hope and said he wasn't coming.

"Then one day an angel appeared to a young woman named Mary. 'You will have a baby boy,' the angel said. 'You shall call him Jesus.'

"'How can I have a child?' asked Mary. 'I'm not married.'

"'Your child will be the holy Son of God,' the angel said. Mary knew then that she would be the mother of the promised Savior.

"After awhile, Jesus was born in a stable. God's Son had come at last! Mary's baby was different from any other baby ever born. He had no earthly father. God was his Father. He must have looked very much like his mother on the outside, but inside he was just like his heavenly Father. Jesus was a man and God at the same time. He was perfect in every way." Mrs. Kendrick stopped.

"That's a great story!" said Jodie. "Please tell it again."

TO DISCUSS

Jesus is the King of Glory. Did he wear his crown on earth? Some paintings show him with a halo (a ring of light) above his head. Did people see a halo on him? What did they see? How did you think his followers knew he was God?

TO DO

Find a Christmas card picture of Jesus in the manger. Glue it to a paper plate. Underneath print, "Jesus, the Son of God." Decorate the edges of the plate, attach a ribbon at the top, and hang it on your wall.

TO PRAY

Thank the Savior for coming into the world.

CHAPTER NINETEEN

Acts 2:22-24

Men of Israel, listen to this: Jesus of Nazareth was a man accredited by God to you by miracles, wonders and signs, which God did among you through him, as you yourselves know. This man was handed over to you by God's set purpose and foreknowledge; and you, with the help of wicked men, put him to death by nailing him to the cross. But God raised him from the dead, freeing him from the agony of death, because it was impossible for death to keep its hold on him. NIV

Jesus' Earthly Life, Death, and Resurrection

Bible Explorers," Mrs. Kendrick said, "let's continue our story about Jesus. While he grew up, he lived with his mother, Mary, and her husband, Joseph. He always obeyed them and never sinned. Why is that?"

"Because he's God, and God never sins," answered Joshua.

"Yes," said Mrs. Kendrick. "When Jesus was about thirty years old, he was baptized, and then he began his ministry. He was kind and loving, showing everyone what God the Father is like. He healed the sick, made blind people see, and he

even raised some dead people. He taught wonderful lessons to his followers. And then he died."

Jodie looked surprised. "He died?" she asked. "I thought you said he's God and lived forever."

"He had to die so we could go to heaven," said Mrs. Kendrick. "Do you remember I told you that the first two people sinned? Since then, every person has been born a sinner. All of us have disobeyed God, which is sin.

God hates sin, and he must punish those who do it. Sinners can't go to heaven but must suffer in hell.

"You see, Jodie, Jesus loves us all so much that he wanted to take our punishment for us," Mrs. Kendrick went on. "His punishment was death on a cross.

"Jesus had awful treatment. People lied about him, spit in his face, placed a crown of thorns on his head, and whipped him on his bare back. They nailed his hands and feet to a cross. For six long hours Jesus hung there, shedding his blood. Then he died, taking the punishment that we deserve."

Tears glistened in Jodie's eyes. "I'm sorry he's dead," she said. "I wish I could have known him."

"But he's not dead now, Jodie," Mike said at once. "Three days after he died, he came back to life."

"That's right!" said Mrs. Kendrick. "Some of Jesus' friends came to the tomb where Jesus was buried. They thought they were going to see Jesus' body, but instead they saw a bright light. 'Do not be afraid,' an angel

said, 'Jesus is not here, he is alive!' Jesus' friends were so excited, they ran to tell everyone."

A big smile came over Jodie's face.

"Many people saw him alive," Mrs. Kendrick continued. "After forty days, his followers saw him rise up from the earth and go back through the clouds to heaven. Someday he'll come back again and take all God's children to heaven."

"I wish I was one of his children," said Jodie. "Will you tell me how, Mrs. Kendrick?" So, while the other children went to play, Jodie trusted Jesus as her Savior.

TO DISCUSS

Why did Jesus come to earth and die on the cross? Read Hebrews 12:2. How did Jesus feel about dying on the cross?

TO DO

Solve the puzzle "Some Things to Remember about Jesus." Fill in the blanks in the sentences, looking up the verses if you need to. (The first two are done for you.) These words are in the puzzle. Beginning at the star, draw from one dot to the next, connecting the words in order. What have you drawn? What does this remind you about Jesus? He _____ me.

Thank Jesus for dying for you and rising again.

Some Things to Remember about Jesus

1. He _showed_ us what God the Father is like (John 14:7).
2. He gave us an _example_ for living (1 Peter 2:21).
3. He never _____ (1 Peter 2:22).
4. He came to destroy the works of the _____ (1 John 3:8).
5. He showed God's _____ for the whole world (John 3:16).
6. He _____ God's truths. (Matthew 5:1-2).
7. He healed the _____, the _____, the _____, and the _____. He _____ the dead. He preached the _____ (Matthew 11:5).
8. He _____ for our sins and _____ again (1 Corinthians 15:3-4).
9. He went back to _____ (Acts 1:9).

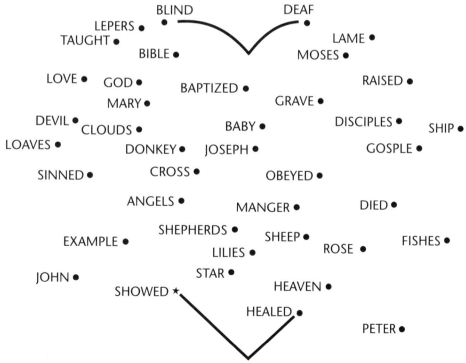

Answer is on page 226.

CHAPTER TWENTY

John 14:16-17
I will ask the Father and he will give you another Comforter, and he will never leave you. He is the Holy Spirit, the Spirit who leads into all truth. TLB

God the Holy Spirit

One dark, stormy night the Kendricks drove into their carport and dashed for the front door. "Oh, we forgot to turn on the outside light," said Mr. Kendrick, fumbling for the door lock. "I can't see the keyhole. Did you bring your flashlight, Betty?"

Mrs. Kendrick quickly reached into her purse, took out a small flashlight, and flicked on the switch. But nothing happened. They were still in the dark. Finally, after everyone was soaked, Dad fitted the key in the lock, and they went inside.

At the Bible Explorers Club the next day, Mrs. Kendrick brought out her flashlight and told everyone what had happened. "What do you suppose was wrong?" she asked.

"Were the batteries worn out?" asked Mike.

"It was worse than that," Mrs. Kendrick said, with a smile. "There were no batteries in the flashlight. I had forgotten that I needed to buy some. This flashlight can be a good object lesson for today's lesson, which is about the God the Holy Spirit. Just as my flashlight needed batteries to have the power to operate, we need the Holy Spirit to help us live the Christian life."

"What is the Holy Spirit like?" asked Jodie.

"Do you remember that we said God is in three persons, and yet he is one God?" Mrs. Kendrick asked. "There is God the Father, God the

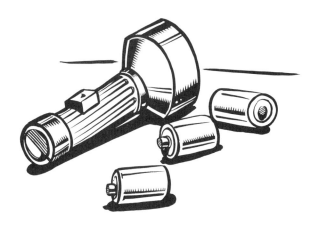

Son, and God the Holy Spirit. Although he is invisible, the Holy Spirit is a person, not a thing. He has lived forever, he knows every-

thing, and he has feelings and a will.

"Before Jesus left this earth, he told his disciples, 'I am going away, but you will not be alone. I will send the Holy Spirit to be your helper. Wait together in Jerusalem until the Holy Spirit comes.'

"Ten days after Jesus went back to heaven, the believers, who were all in an upper room, heard the sound of a mighty, rushing wind. What looked like tiny flames of fire appeared above each head. From that time on, the Holy Spirit lived within them, and they became powerful witnesses for God."

"The Holy Spirit is inside us, isn't he?" Sara asked.

"Yes," answered Mrs. Kendrick, "he comes to live in us when we trust Jesus as our Savior. He gives us the power to live the Christian life. Without him, we would fail. The Holy Spirit teaches us about God and helps us understand the Bible when we read it. He helps us to pray, and he even prays for us when we have trouble finding the right words. He helps us love God and obey him."

"Dad taught us in our Sunday school class about the fruit of the Spirit," Joshua said. "He said the Holy Spirit will grow the fruit of love, joy, peace, goodness, and things like that in our lives, if we'll let him be in charge."

"I think the Holy Spirit is really working on Mom and Dad," said Mike. "They've promised to go to church next Sunday."

"We'll pray that he'll keep on talking to your folks until soon they'll trust Jesus."

TO DISCUSS

When you sin, how does the Holy Spirit feel? (Look up Ephesians 4:30.) What do you need the Holy Spirit to do for you today? If you are a Christian, what can you do to receive his help? What are the two best ways of finding out how to please the Holy Spirit?

TO DO

Read Galatians 5:22-23. Draw a large bunch of nine grapes and label each grape with the nine good things the Holy Spirit gives us.

TO PRAY

Ask the Holy Spirit to develop his fruit in your life for the glory of Christ.

PART 5

What God Does

KEY MEMORY VERSES

Psalm 86:8-10

Among the gods there is none like You, O Lord;
Nor are there any works like Your works.
All nations whom You have made
Shall come and worship before You, O Lord,
And shall glorify Your name.
For You are great, and do wondrous things;
You alone are God. *NKJV*

CHAPTER TWENTY-ONE

Hebrews 1:10

Lord, in the beginning you made the earth, and the heavens are the work of your hands. TLB

How Did the Universe Get Here?

Bible Explorers, here are crayons and paper," Mrs. Kendrick said. "Each of you draw a picture of plants, animals, and people. Your picture will help us learn something about today's lesson." When they were done, everyone said Jodie's picture was best.

"What materials did you need for drawing your pictures?" Mrs. Kendrick asked.

"Crayons and paper," answered Sara.

"Could you make a picture if you had no materials?"

Sara shook her head. "No. I can't make something from nothing. Nobody can."

"God did," declared Joshua.

"Yes," said his mom. "Our new theme is 'The Works of God.' Today's lesson is 'How Did the

Universe Get Here?' People can make some marvelous things, but they must have some kind of material from which to make them. When God made our whole universe, he made it from nothing. He spoke, and it was there."

Mrs. Kendrick held up Jodie's picture. "This is pretty," she went on. "I would like to hang it up. Perhaps it could go here," she said, holding the picture in the air and letting go. The picture fell to the ground. "It wouldn't stay in the air. Why is that?"

"You can't hang it in the air," said Mike. "Gravity won't let you. You have to fasten it to something."

"The Bible says God hung our earth on nothing," said Mrs. Kendrick. "You drew a picture of a tiger, Josh. Could you turn that tiger into a living, breathing tiger?"

Joshua shook his head. "No one can make a living thing," he said.

"That's right," said Mrs. Kendrick. "Aren't you glad that God made our universe? Shall we thank him now for this wonderful work of his hands?"

TO DISCUSS

Before God created the universe, was there any air? Any light? Any spark of life? What was there? In the beginning, when there was nothing, what did God do? (Quote Genesis 1:1 for your answer.)

TO DO

On a piece of paper, draw a picture similar to the ones drawn by the Bible Explorers. On the back of your paper, write these statements:
1. I needed paper and crayons—God made the earth from nothing.
2. I can only draw pictures—God made living things.
3. I must hang my picture on something—God hung the world on nothing.

TO PRAY

Thank God for his perfect work of creating the universe and everything in it, including you.

CHAPTER TWENTY-TWO

Genesis 1:27
So God created man in His own image; in the image of God He created him; male and female He created them. NKJV

Hebrews 11:3
By faith we understand that the universe was formed at God's command. NIV

God Created Man

One Saturday morning Mrs. Kendrick took the Bible Explorers to the zoo. They looked at many animals and birds. They loved watching the monkeys on monkey island. As people held food over a wall, some of the monkeys tried to cross a water-filled moat to get it.

"Look at that big fellow over there," said Mike. "He acts like he's afraid to get wet. See how he holds his hands over his head and sort of tiptoes across?"

"Yeah, but that scrawny little monkey isn't afraid," said Joshua. "He splashes through the water and doesn't care how wet he gets."

"Say, Joshua, which kind of monkey did you descend from?" asked Jodie. She pointed to a big baboon in a nearby cage. "Maybe he's one of your

97

relatives," she added, with a laugh. "Hey, look at what Joshua's great-great grandpa looked like!" she yelled. With that, all the children tried to find just the right "relative" for someone else.

After lunch, the Bible Explorers began their lesson. "Many people believe the theory that people came from monkeys," said Mrs. Kendrick.

"My schoolteacher believes in evolution," said Mike. "He says that everything began many billions of years ago with a one-celled tiny creature in the sea and that through time, new forms developed by chance out of other forms. Finally, there were monkeys, and then people."

"Evolution is only a theory—a belief that has never been proven," said Mrs. Kendrick.

"The Bible says that God created each type of creature," said Mrs. Kendrick. "One creature can't become or produce any other kind of creature."

Joshua grinned at Jodie. "See there?" he said. "No baboon was my great-great grandpa."

Mrs. Kendrick smiled. "Also," she went on, "of all God's creation, only man is made in God's image. When God breathed life into Adam, Adam became a living soul who would never die. When animals die, they are gone forever. Also, we are different from the animals because we can talk and think. We can decide to do right or wrong."

"And best of all, we can trust Jesus and be saved," said Mike.

TO DISCUSS

How does the Bible say that Adam and Eve were created? Of everything that God created, what creatures can choose between right and wrong?

TO DO

Look up Genesis 1:1-11. At the top of a piece of paper write, "Who started everything?" and at the bottom write, "God did!" Fill the rest of the sheet with pictures of things God created, including Adam and Eve.

TO PRAY

Thank God for all the wonderful people he created, including you.

Nehemiah 9:6
You alone are the Lord;
You have made heaven,
The heaven of heavens, with
  all their host,
The earth and everything on it,
The seas and all that is in
  them,
And You preserve them all.
The host of heaven worships
  You. NKJV

God Is in Charge of Nature

It was a wild, stormy night. Rains poured from the sky, and the wind whipped through the trees. There were bright streaks of lightning and loud, booming thunder. Joshua got out of bed and hurried to his parents' room. "I'm scared," he told them. "May I stay in here with you?"

"Let's all go to the living room and wait out the storm," said Dad. Suddenly the lights went out. With only a flashlight to see by, the family huddled together on the sofa and prayed for the Lord's protection.

Suddenly there was a tapping sound on the roof and windows. "What's that?" asked Joshua.

"It's hail," Dad replied. "What a storm!" In another hour, the storm passed. After looking over the house and going outside to see the ankle-deep hailstones,

everyone went back to bed, thankful that the Lord had kept them safe.

That afternoon, at the Bible Explorers meeting, the children all told of their experiences during the storm. Then Mrs. Kendrick said, "We can thank the Lord that he protected us all from harm. We must always remember one thing: God is in charge of nature."

"Well, then, why does he let bad things happen, like that storm?" asked Jodie.

"My science book says that storms are good for the land, even though they do some harm," said Mike. "We need the rain, and lightning causes natural fires in the forests that help to keep down too much undergrowth."

"That's right," agreed Mrs. Kendrick. "God knows what is best for his creation. He has created laws for the universe, which he has made. There is the law of gravity, which keeps us from flying out into space. He created a magnetic force, which causes compass needles to point north. Because of his laws, the earth and other planets stay in their orbits, the oceans don't flood the earth, and so on."

"But one time he flooded the whole earth," said Sara. "Does that mean he can change his laws when he wants to?"

Mrs. Kendrick nodded. "Yes," she said. "God made the earth, and he can change its laws if he chooses to do so. But he promised never to flood the entire earth again, and he placed a rainbow in the sky to remind us of that. If God quit taking care of our universe, even for a few seconds, there would be disaster everywhere. Aren't you glad he's in charge?"

"I sure am," said Jodie. "It makes me feel so safe."

TO DISCUSS

When God changes the laws of nature, it is called a miracle. Can you name some of his miracles? What would happen if God suspended the law of gravity? If he caused the earth to move closer to the sun, what would occur?

TO DO

On a piece of paper, draw a rainbow. Underneath it print, "God's sign that he will never destroy the whole earth again by a flood." Draw a sun and a moon and beneath them print, "God will keep these in their places to give us our days, our months, and our years."

TO PRAY

Thank the Lord that he is in charge of nature. Ask him to protect you throughout this day.

CHAPTER TWENTY-FOUR

Proverbs 14:34
Righteousness exalts a nation, but sin is a disgrace to any people. NIV

God Is in Charge of the Nations

One day Joshua and Mike took a trip into the city with Joshua's dad. As they walked along a downtown street, they saw a dirty, ragged man sitting with his back against a wall. "Sir, will you help a poor, homeless soldier?" he asked Mr. Kendrick.

Mr. Kendrick walked over to the man. "Did you fight in a war?" he asked. "Yes, sir. I am a Vietnam veteran," the man answered. "Ever since I came back from the war, nothing has gone right. Now I can't get a job, and nobody seems to care."

Mr. Kendrick handed the soldier some money and a business card. "Here is a little money to help out," he said. "If you want a job, go to this address. I know that the head of that company likes to hire veterans." Then Mr. Kendrick talked to the man about Jesus.

105

WHAT GOD DOES

At the next Bible Explorers meeting, Mike and Joshua told the others about the homeless man. "I hope he gets a job," said Joshua. "I think it's terrible that any of our country's soldiers could be homeless like that."

"Me, too," said Mike. "I think wars are awful. Mrs. Kendrick, why doesn't God stop countries from having wars? He could do it if he wanted to, couldn't he?"

"God wants to bless countries and all the people in them," said Mrs. Kendrick, "but he will not bless those who disobey him. He disciplines people for their own good, so they'll learn not to sin. You see, when people sin, they are really hurting themselves or others—even if they don't know it at the time."

"If everyone obeyed God, there wouldn't be wars and other bad troubles. Right?" said Mike.

"You're right, Mike," said Mrs. Kendrick. "God is in charge of the nations. He is the great Ruler over all the earth. He gives each nation, and each person in a nation, the chance to choose between right and wrong. If they choose to do wrong, they bring troubles on themselves."

"I know when there'll be peace over the earth," said Joshua. "It's

when Jesus comes back and rules over the world. Then he won't let people hurt each other, will he?"

"No," answered Mrs. Kendrick. "He won't allow anyone to sin then. Someday all nations must bow before Jesus and recognize him as the King of kings. Until then, we must pray for our nation and its leaders and obey the Lord ourselves. Perhaps, for our sakes, he will spare our nation from trouble."

TO DISCUSS

Why do wars and other bad things happen? If people keep on disobeying God, what will finally happen to them? (Read Romans 2:5.) When will there be peace on the earth forever?

TO DO

Work the puzzle on the next page, "God Is in Charge of the Nations."

TO PRAY

Thank the Lord for your country. Ask him to give wisdom to its leaders. Ask him to help you do your part for your country by living to please him.

God Is in Charge of the Nations

Draw a line through the maze. On the blanks below, write the letters in order as you find them. Then separate the letters into words.

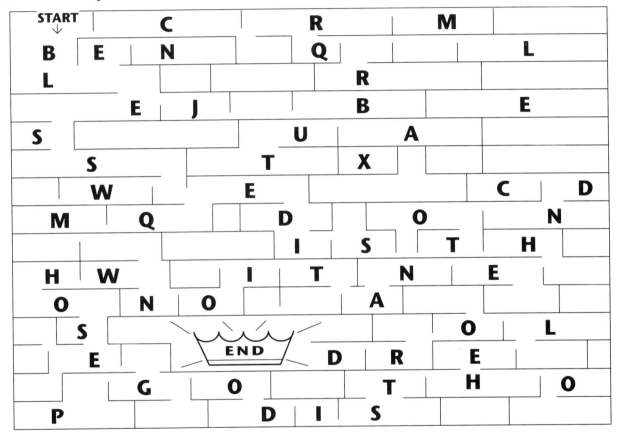

"___ ___ ___ ___ ___ ___ ___ ___ ___ ___ ___ ___ ___ ___ ___ ___"

___ ___ ___ ___ ___ ___ ___ ___ ___ ___ ___ ___ ___ ___ ___ ___.

Psalm 33:12

Answer is on page 227.

CHAPTER TWENTY-FIVE

1 Peter 3:10-13

If you want a happy, good life, keep control of your tongue, and guard your lips from telling lies. Turn away from evil and do good. Try to live in peace even if you must run after it to catch and hold it! For the Lord is watching his children, listening to their prayers; but the Lord's face is hard against those who do evil. TLB

Is God in Charge of You?

"Hey, Josh," said Max, as Joshua walked up to a group of boys, "we're going swimming. Want to come?"

"I'd like to," Joshua said, "but I can't. My folks won't let me go when there are no adults along."

"That's nothing," said Max. "My parents wouldn't let me, either, if I'd ask them—which I'm not going to do. Come on! Your folks will never know."

Joshua shook his head. "No," he stated firmly. "I try to obey, whether my parents know what I'm doing or not."

"Poor itty, bitty baby," said Max with a snicker. "He has to obey his mommy. Little Joshua always clings to his mommy's apron strings!" The boys walked away. Joshua felt awful.

When Joshua got home, he took out his tape

recorder and listened to a recording which his grandfather had made for him several years ago. Later, at the Bible Explorers meeting, Joshua told about the boys' teasing. "Listening to Grandpa's tape helped me," he said. "On it he told me that God is in charge of every person. He doesn't make us do right, but he lets us choose what we'll do. Then he tells us that he will bless those who obey him."

"That's what Joshua's grandpa—who was my father—lived by," Mrs. Kendrick told the class. "When I was growing up, we were poor. More than once Father could have made more money

in his business if he had cheated and lied. But he always chose to do right. He'd tell us, 'God's in charge. He'll take care of us.' And God always did. Later, God blessed my father with a successful business."

"My folks sure need to be saved and obey God," said Mike. "They fuss and fight, and they're having a lot of trouble. I told them that things would be different if they'd get saved."

"You're right," said Mrs. Kendrick. "Both Christians and sinners have problems and hard times in life. But God's children can turn to him for help."

"God loves every person," Mrs. Kendrick continued. "He wants to bless us all and make us happy. Still, he can't let people sin and get by with it. If you think the kids who do wrong are having more fun than you are, just wait. Their fun won't last forever."

"I like obeying God," said Joshua. "Sometimes it's hard, but I know God wants what is best for me."

TO DISCUSS

Does God have a right to tell each person how to live? Can you give some reasons for your answer? Do sinners ever have fun? Read Hebrews 11:25 to see how long their fun lasts. Who is in charge of what happens to everyone when their lives are over? When is the best time to let God take charge of your life?

TO DO

Read Psalm 1, which tells about the righteous (God's children) and the wicked (sinners). Memorize verse 6 and write it on a piece of paper.

TO PRAY

Thank God that he loves you and wants to do good things for you. Ask him to help you live so that he can bless you.

PART 6

Angels— Good and Bad

KEY MEMORY VERSES

Psalm 91:11-12

For He shall give His angels charge over you,
To keep you in all your ways.
In their hands they shall bear you up,
Lest you dash your foot against a stone. *NKJV*

CHAPTER TWENTY-SIX

Psalm 148:1-5

Praise the Lord!
Praise the Lord from the
heavens;
Praise Him in the heights!
Praise Him, all His angels;
Praise Him, all His hosts!
Praise Him, sun and moon;
Praise Him, all you stars of
light!
Praise Him, you heavens of
heavens,
And you waters above the
heavens!
Let them praise the name of
the Lord,
For He commanded and they
were created. NKJV

The Bible Tells about Angels

Mike's little sister, Kay, loved to look at the pictures in her Bible-story book that Mrs. Kendrick had given her. "Who is that?" she asked Mike one day, pointing to an angel.

"That's an angel," Mike told her.

"Read me the story 'bout the angel," Kay begged. So Mike read her the story of the angel Gabriel, who told Mary she would be the mother of Jesus. Then Kay found another picture of angels. "More angels," she said. "Read me that story."

At the next Bible Explorers lesson, Mrs. Kendrick said, "Our next five lessons will be about angels."

"That's good," said Mike. "Kay loves stories

about angels. She keeps asking about them, but I can't answer her questions."

"We can all learn more," said Mrs. Kendrick. "Angels are real, even though we can't see them. There are probably some in this room right now." The startled children looked all about them. "If we could see the invisible spirit world around us, we'd be amazed," Mrs. Kendrick went on.

"There are both good and bad angels. We'll learn where they came from and what they do."

"Have angels lived forever, like God?" asked Jodie.

"No, angels were created by God," said Mrs. Kendrick. "We don't know when, but it was before God created the earth. All of you look at Job 38:4-7 and see what the angels did when God made the earth."

Sara found the answer first. "They shouted for joy," she said. "Aunt Betty, how many angels are there? Maybe hundreds?"

"The Bible says there are more than we can count," answered Mrs. Kendrick.

"Do they look like the pictures in Kay's book?" asked Mike. "And why can't we see them?"

"Angels are invisible to us," Mrs. Kendrick said. "But in Bible days, they sometimes appeared to people and delivered messages from God. Can you imagine how surprised you'd be if an angel appeared with a message from God?"

Jodie giggled. "That's probably why the angel told Mary not to be afraid. I bet Mary was surprised!"

"That's right," said Mrs. Kendrick. "Here are a few more facts about them: They are wise and powerful, but not all-wise and all-powerful like God. They can travel with great speed. They are neither male or female, and they never marry. The good angels help us. We'll learn about that in our next lesson."

"Isn't this fun?" asked Mike. "I can't wait until our next lesson. And I already have lots to tell Kay."

TO DISCUSS

Look up these verses about angels and answer the questions:
1. Who created the angels (Colossians 1:16)?
2. Find the names of two angels in Daniel 12:1 and Luke 1:26.
3. Name two ways in which angels are greater than we are (2 Peter 2:11).
4. What does 2 Samuel 14:20 say about angels?

TO DO

On a piece of paper, draw a picture of your family and then draw a picture of some angels. At the bottom of the page write, "God's angels help us."

TO PRAY

Thank God for telling us in his Word about angels.

CHAPTER TWENTY-SEVEN

Psalm 91:9-12

For Jehovah is my refuge! I choose the God above all gods to shelter me. How then can evil overtake me or any plague come near? For he orders his angels to protect you wherever you go. They will steady you with their hands to keep you from stumbling against the rocks on the trail. TLB

What Do Good Angels Do?

One day Mike and Joshua took a walk in the woods behind Mike's house, looking for blackberries. "Dad says there are some bushes back here just loaded with berries," Mike said.

"Look, there's lots of them," said Joshua, pointing to his left. As the boys turned, something dashed out of the bushes, right in their path. "What was that?" asked Joshua, jumping back. Both boys stopped dead in their tracks to look.

"Oh, it's just a little bunny," said Mike, with a laugh.

But Joshua saw something else. "Oh no!" said Joshua. "Don't take another step, Mike. There's a rattlesnake!" The boys backed slowly out of the woods and ran back to Mike's house.

"If that bunny hadn't jumped out in front of us,

119

we would have stepped on that rattlesnake!" Mike said as he tried to catch his breath.

"Yeah," said Joshua, "that rabbit saved our lives."

Later, at the Bible Explorers meeting, the boys told about the bunny and the snake. "We thank the Lord for protecting you," said Mrs. Kendrick. "Perhaps it was your guardian angels who sent that bunny scampering across your path.

You see, the Bible tells us that angels guard and protect God's children. When we reach heaven, we may be surprised to learn of the many times that we were protected from danger by them.

"The word *angel* means 'messenger,'" Mrs. Kendrick continued. "Angels are God's messengers. Many stories in the Bible tell about how angels carried God's messages to godly men and women."

"Angels told the shepherds about Baby Jesus," said Jodie.

"Yes, and at the tomb of Jesus, angels told the women that he had risen," added Sara.

"Angels took care of Jesus in the wilderness after Satan tempted him," said Joshua. "They brought him food and water because he had been fasting for forty days and nights."

"In Kay's picture book there is a story about an angel helping Peter escape from prison," Mike said.

"Even though we can't see them, the Bible promises that angels guard and protect us," said Mrs. Kendrick.

"If angels did cause that bunny to jump out at us, I wish I'd seen them do it," said Mike.

"Me, too!" said Joshua.

TO DISCUSS

Can you tell of an experience of yours when you were in danger but were not harmed? Of course, God helped you, but what might he have used to keep you safe? What does the word *angel* mean?

TO DO

Solve the puzzle on the next page, "God's Wonderful Angels."

TO PRAY

Thank the Lord for your guardian angel.

God's Wonderful Angels

Write the letter missing from each set. What do we call the angel who watches over you?

R S T U V W X Z

L M N P Q R S T

O P Q R S T V W

Q S T U V W X Y

A B C D E F H I

P Q R S T V W X

Y Z B C D E F G

K L M N O P Q S

C E F G H I J K

D E F G H J K L

T U V W X Y Z B

M O P Q R S T U

Z B C D E F G H

I J K L M O P Q

D E F H I J K L

A B C D F G H I

J K M N O P Q R

A B C D E F G H I J K L M N O P Q R S T U V W X Y Z

Answer is on page 228.

CHAPTER TWENTY-EIGHT

Isaiah 14:12-15

How you are fallen from heaven, O Lucifer, son of the morning! How you are cut down to the ground—mighty though you were against the nations of the world. For you said to yourself, "I will ascend to heaven and rule the angels. I will take the highest throne I will . . . be like the Most High." But instead, you will be brought down to the pit of hell, down to its lowest depth. TLB

What about Bad Angels?

Mrs. Kendrick, you told us that there are good and bad angels," Mike said. "Well, who are the bad angels? Could any of them be here in this room with us, like good angels are?"

"I know who the bad angels are," said Joshua, before his mother could answer. "They're Satan and his demons. Right?"

"Yes," answered Mrs. Kendrick. "We'll talk about them today. And yes, Mike, some of them could be here now."

"Well, how did they come to be?" asked Jodie. "You told us that God never made anything bad. So who made bad angels?"

"They made themselves bad," Mrs. Kendrick told her. "When God made the angels, they were all pure and good. But, like people, God made them with the ability to choose whether to do right or wrong. One very beautiful and wise angel was Lucifer, whose name means 'day-star.' He was a commander, or leader, of other angels.

123

"Lucifer became very proud because of his wisdom and beauty. He grew jealous of God and wanted to be greater than God. He wanted to be worshiped. 'I will raise my throne above the stars of God, I will be like the most High,' he said. Because of his great sin, Lucifer was thrown out of heaven and became Satan, the devil."

"Well, who are the demons?" Mike wanted to know.

"They are the angels who followed Lucifer and rebelled against God. They let him be their leader, and they, too, were forced to leave heaven," Mrs. Kendrick said. "Now they do the wicked things that Satan tells them to do. Satan cannot be everywhere at once, as God can. But Satan sends his demons all over the world to do his work."

"What does Satan look like?" asked Sara. "Is he red all over with a tail and horns and carrying a pitchfork?"

Mrs. Kendrick laughed. "That's just some artist's idea of the devil," she said. "Satan is invisible. Neither that artist nor anyone else has seen him. I'm sure, though, that his wickedness has caused him to lose most of his former beauty. What we do know from the Bible is that he changes himself to seem like an angel of light when he tempts us. What do you think that means?"

"Well, he makes us think that sinning would be fun and wouldn't get us into trouble," said Mike. "But if we listen to him and sin, we'll find that sinning does hurt us."

"He's not really an angel of light; he's a liar," said Mrs. Kendrick. "Always remember that when you're tempted to sin."

TO DISCUSS

Read Genesis 2:17. What did God say would happen to Adam and Eve if they ate the forbidden fruit? Now look at what the serpent (Satan) told Eve in Genesis 3:4. When Eve looked at the fruit, did Satan seem like an angel of light or a liar? When she and Adam ate the fruit, what did they find out that Satan really was?

TO DO

On a piece of paper, draw a stick figure to represent Satan. Around him, draw rays of light. As in a cartoon drawing, show him saying, "Steal that dollar." Next to him, draw a stick figure representing yourself, saying, "No, Satan, you are a liar. I will ask Jesus to make you go away."

TO PRAY

Ask the Lord to help you stay close to him today and not to be fooled by Satan's temptations.

CHAPTER TWENTY-NINE

1 Peter 5:8

Be self-controlled and alert. Your enemy the devil prowls around like a roaring lion looking for someone to devour.

NIV

1 John 4:4

Dear young friends, you belong to God and have already won your fight with those who are against Christ because there is someone in your hearts who is stronger than any evil teacher in this wicked world. TLB

What Do Bad Angels Do?

Mrs. Kendrick held up the picture of a zebra, who was peacefully grazing, unaware that a lion was stalking him. "Bible Explorers, what is this lion planning to do?" she asked.

"He'll try to get close to the zebra, and then he'll pounce on him and kill him," said Mike.

"The Bible tells about someone who goes around like a roaring lion, seeking whom he may devour," said Mrs. Kendrick, putting down the picture. "It is the devil, and we are warned to be very watchful of him. A lion may roar when he is hungry. But when he begins to stalk his prey, of course, he is silent, hoping to sneak up on him. That's the way the devil works. He makes you think sin would be fun. He never tells you how harmful it is.

"Today we will talk about what the bad angels

127

do," Mrs. Kendrick continued. "In Jesus' day, the demons entered the bodies of people and made them do terrible things. What did Jesus do to help those people?"

"He threw the demons out," answered Sara. "Can demons live in people today?"

"They can never live inside God's children," answered Mrs. Kendrick. "But they do sometimes live in sinners, especially in lands where the devil is worshiped by many people.

What else do Satan and the demons do?"

"I know they try to keep us from getting saved," said Mike.

"What about fortune-tellers and horoscopes and stuff like that?" asked Joshua. "Don't the demons use them?"

"Yes," said Mrs. Kendrick, "and at séances, where people think they're hearing dead people speak, they're really hearing demons. The Bible says we must never have anything to do

with witches or fortune-tellers. Stay away from such people."

"Daddy told me not to play with Ouija boards," said Sara. "He said they're used in demon worship."

"Yes, that's right," said Mrs. Kendrick. "Most of all, watch out for Satan's temptations. He can't make you sin or steal you away from God, but he is always sneaking around, tempting you to do wrong. You're not strong enough to fight off that old lion by yourself. Who is stronger than Satan?"

"Jesus!" said Sara. "When Satan tempts me to do wrong, I say, 'Jesus, the old devil is bothering me. Chase him away.' And Jesus will do it."

"Love and obey Jesus always," Mrs. Kendrick said. "Pray and read your Bible every day. Then, you'll have God's help in winning your fights against the devil."

TO DISCUSS

Who are your greatest enemies? Are you as powerful as Satan? Who is more powerful than he is? How can you protect yourself from Satan's fiery darts—his temptations (Ephesians 6:16)? What do you think that means? What weapon do we have to fight Satan (Ephesians 6:17)?

TO DO

On a piece of paper, draw a stick figure, representing yourself. Show darts with fire on the tips coming in your direction. Draw a box around you, with its sides labeled, "prayer," "faith in God," and "reading God's Word." Underneath, write, "The way to put out Satan's fiery darts."

TO PRAY

Thank the Lord that you don't have to fight Satan by yourself. Ask him to help you win victories over Satan and sin today.

CHAPTER THIRTY

What Will Happen to the Angels?

Revelation 5:11-12

Then I looked and heard the voice of many angels, numbering thousands upon thousands, and ten thousand times ten thousand. They encircled the throne and the living creatures and the elders. In a loud voice they sang:

"Worthy is the Lamb, who was slain, to receive power and wealth and wisdom and strength and honor and glory and praise!" NIV

"Aunt Betty, does the devil live in hell?" Sara asked Mrs. Kendrick one day. "Does he come to earth to tempt us and then go back there for his home?"

"No, he doesn't live there now, Sara," answered Mrs. Kendrick. "We'll talk about that today at Bible Explorers Club. You go find the other children, and we'll begin our lesson."

"We're going to talk about where the devil lives," Sara told the others when they came together. "I've heard people talk about him being in hell, spitting fire, but Aunt Betty says he doesn't live there."

"There are many false ideas about Satan," said Mrs. Kendrick. "The Bible says that after he sinned against God, he was no longer the

131

commander of the good angels, and heaven was not his home. He is called the 'Prince of the power of the air.' As the ruler of the evil angels, the demons, he has his headquarters in the air above us."

"Yeah, but he and his demons come to earth when they tempt people, don't they?" asked Mike.

"They were here in Jesus' day," said Joshua, "because Jesus cast them out of some people."

"Oh yes, the devil and his helpers are free to roam about as they wish on the earth now," said Mrs. Kendrick. "But a day is coming when they will be punished. When Jesus comes again to rule over this earth for a thousand years, he will chain up Satan so that he can't harm or tempt anyone. After the thousand years, Satan and all his demons will be punished in the lake of fire, called hell, forever and ever."

"I wish they were locked up in hell right now," said Mike. "Without them around, it would be a lot easier to be good."

"Mike, the devil and his demons can be just as powerless to hurt you now as they will be then, if you will let Jesus rule in your heart," Mrs. Kendrick told him. "You must let Jesus help you and every day ask him to help you resist Satan. He is powerful, but Jesus is all-powerful."

"What will happen to the good angels?" asked Jodie.

"They will always live in heaven, worshiping and serving God," answered Mrs. Kendrick. "Won't it be wonderful to see all those millions of angels, gathered around Jesus' throne?"

"When I get to heaven, I think it would be neat to find out who my guardian angel is," said Joshua.

"I want to see the angels," said Jodie, "but most of all, I want to see Jesus." And all the others agreed.

TO DISCUSS

Why did God make hell? Does he want people to go there? What did he do so we wouldn't have to go there? Read James 4:7 and find two things you must do to cause Satan to run away from you.

TO DO

Jesus quoted Scripture when Satan tempted him. Below are two lists. The first list names some things Satan might tempt you to do. The second list gives Scriptures that you can use to resist Satan. Look up the Scriptures, and draw a line from each one to the temptation it fits.

1. Steal a dollar.
2. Tell a lie.
3. Disobey your parents.
4. Complain about going to church.
5. Wish you owned your friend's bike.

A. Ephesians 6:1
B. Exodus 20:17
C. Psalm 122:1
D. Ephesians 4:28
E. Colossians 3:9

TO PRAY

Thank the Lord that he is more powerful than Satan. Ask him to help you resist the devil today.

Answer is on page 229.

PART 7

We Are Sinners

Romans 3:23

For all have sinned and fall short of the glory of God.

NKJV

CHAPTER THIRTY-ONE

Genesis 1:31
*God saw all that he had
made, and it was very
good. . . .* NIV

Did God Make Adam Good or Bad?

One day when Joshua was in town, a man stopped him and said, "Excuse me. You look just like somebody I went to school with many years ago. His name was Joshua Kendrick. Are you related to him?"

Joshua looked surprised. "I'm Joshua Kendrick," he said. "But you didn't go to school with me."

The man laughed. "No, I'm sure I'm much too old for that. But is your father named Joshua, too?"

"Oh yes," said Joshua. "Really, I'm Joshua Kendrick, Jr."

"I just knew you must be related," said the man.

"With your black hair and blue eyes, you look so much like your dad did in grammar school. You walk and talk like him, too."

When Joshua proudly told the other Bible Explorers about meeting the man, his mother said, "That reminds me of a recent lesson we had. Do you remember when we said that God made Adam and Eve—and all people—in his likeness? Does that mean that people look like God in outward appearance?"

"No," answered Jodie, "but we can talk and think. That's one way we're like God."

"And we can choose right or wrong," added Mike. "And our souls will never die."

"Right," said Mrs. Kendrick. "In those, and in other ways, people are made in God's image. Everything God

made was good, yet we know that Adam and Eve sinned. How did they get that way? Did God make sinners? The answer is no. When God made the first two people, they were pure and innocent of sin. But, unlike God, they could sin. They could choose to obey him, or to disobey."

"And they disobeyed, didn't they?" asked Sara.

"Yes, they did, Sara," said Mrs. Kendrick. "All of you know the story. God told Adam and Eve not to eat the fruit on the tree of knowledge of good and evil. One day Satan, in the form of a serpent, tempted Eve to eat the fruit. She ate it and offered some to Adam, who ate it, too."

"Yeah, God made them good, but they made themselves bad," added Joshua.

"If they had never sinned, everything would have been perfect for them forever," said Mrs. Kendrick. "Instead, terrible things happened because of sin. We will talk about that in our next lesson."

TO DISCUSS

Has someone ever said that you look like one of your parents? Adam and Eve were made in God's image. How were they like God? After they sinned, were they like God in purity? What had they become?

TO DO

On a piece of paper, draw four hearts. Leave numbers one and four white. Shade numbers two and three gray and draw black spots (sins) on them. Write the following words under each, as indicated: (1) God made Adam and

WE ARE SINNERS

Eve pure and good. (2) Adam and Eve made themselves sinners. (3) I was born a sinner. I have sinned. (4) Jesus' blood washes a sinner's heart clean.

TO PRAY

Thank God that, although you have sinned, Jesus died to take away your sins.

CHAPTER THIRTY-TWO

When Adam Sinned

Ecclesiastes 11:9

Young man, it's wonderful to be young! Enjoy every minute of it! Do all you want to; take in everything, but realize that you must account to God for everything you do. TLB

Jeremiah 5:25

And so I have taken away these wondrous blessings from them. This sin has robbed them of all of these good things. TLB

Joshua pressed his nose to the car window as they neared Grandpa's farm. It was Friday night, and Joshua was staying at Grandpa's. He liked to help Grandpa with the evening chores.

That evening Joshua and Grandpa worked hard. As Joshua was getting ready for bed, he heard the frightened cackling of chickens. "Grandpa!" he yelled, dashing toward the front of the house. "Come quick! There's something bothering the chickens!"

Grabbing his flashlight, Grandpa ran outside, closely followed by Joshua. They found the door of the henhouse slightly ajar, and inside there was pandemonium. Frightened chickens flapped their wings, jostled against each other, and squawked loudly.

"I can't see what's causing the commotion," said Grandpa, shining his light all around. Then he flashed a beam into the yard. "There's the trouble!" he exclaimed, pointing to a possum, trotting away with a chicken in its mouth. "You must have left the door open when you fed the chickens, Joshua," he said. "Please be more careful next time."

A few days later, Joshua told the Bible Explorers about the possum. "That chicken-stealing animal is a good illustration of what happened when Adam and Eve sinned," said Mrs. Kendrick. "Joshua left the henhouse door open, giving the possum a chance to get at the chickens. Eve opened the door to the devil by listening to him and looking longingly at the fruit. What happened when the possum got into the henhouse?"

"One of Grandpa's best hens was killed," answered Joshua.

His mother nodded. "God had warned Adam that trouble would come if they ate the forbidden fruit, and it did. First of all, Adam and Eve were ashamed because they realized they were naked. They ran to hide behind some trees. But, of course, they couldn't hide from God.

"Their fellowship with God was broken. Inside, in their hearts, they were no longer pure and innocent of sin. Instead, they had a sinful nature, which means they had a desire to sin. Their own bodies were different, for now they would suffer pain and sickness and would eventually die.

"The entire world was changed. Thorns and thistles began to grow, and Adam had to work hard to make a living. The animals, who had been

docile and friendly, became wild and hostile. Man's sin allowed Satan to influence the world and become its god and prince."

"Children," Mrs. Kendrick went on, "God doesn't force people to obey him. They can go ahead and sin if they want to, but sin always brings terrible consequences. When you realize you are being tempted to do wrong, don't open the door to the devil, not even a tiny crack. Ask God to help you say no to sin always."

TO DISCUSS

What are some ways we open the door to the devil? What can we do to keep the door shut tight against his attacks?

TO DO

Solve the word search puzzle "The Results of Sin."

TO PRAY

Ask the Lord to help you say no to Satan's temptations so that you won't need to suffer the consequences of sin.

The Results of Sin

Find the underlined words in the word search puzzle. (The word sin will be there five times.) Go across or down only.

1. At first Adam and Eve were pure and **innocent** of **sin**.
2. After their **sin**, the ground had **thorns** and **thistles**.
3. God said they would **die**.
4. They began to have **pain** and **sickness**.
5. The animals became wild and **hostile**.
6. Adam had to work hard to make a **living**.
7. Adam and Eve had to leave their **home** in the garden.
8. Now they had a **nature** that wanted to **sin**.
9. **Sin** will take away **good** things from **me**.
10. With God's help, I will say **no** to **sin**.

T	H	I	S	T	L	E	S
H	O	S	T	I	L	E	I
O	M	S	H	N	G	X	C
M	E	I	O	N	O	X	K
S	I	N	R	O	O	S	N
P	A	I	N	C	D	I	E
S	I	N	S	E	X	N	S
L	I	V	I	N	G	O	S
S	I	N	A	T	U	R	E

Answer is on page 229.

We All Have Sinned

Romans 3:10-12, 23

As it is written:
"There is none righteous, no,
*   not one;*
There is none who understands;
There is none who seeks after
*   God.*
They have all turned aside;
They have together become
*   unprofitable;*
There is none who does good,
*   no, not one. . . ."*
For all have sinned and fall
*   short of the glory of God.*

NKJV

Mike was taking care of his little sister, Kay, one day when it was time for Bible Explorers Club, so he brought her along with him. He was early, so he left Kay in the living room for a few minutes while he went with Joshua to get a drink of water. Suddenly there was a sound of breaking glass. "What was that?" asked Mrs. Kendrick, coming into the kitchen.

"I don't know, but I think it came from the living room," said Mike. "Kay is in there." Mrs. Kendrick and Mike rushed into the living room, and on the floor was a vase, smashed into tiny pieces. Kay was standing in a far corner of the room, looking frightened.

"I didn't do it," said Kay. "I was over here. It just fell off the table and busted."

"Are you sure you didn't give it a little push?" asked Mike. No matter how hard Mike tried to get his sister to admit she had broken the vase, she wouldn't do it.

When the girls arrived for the lesson, Mrs.

Kendrick told them about the vase. "Mike, did you teach Kay to lie?" she asked. "Did your parents?"

Mike looked a little shocked. "Of course not," he said. "We wouldn't do that."

"Then how do you suppose she learned to do it?" Mrs. Kendrick asked.

"It's something inside of us that just comes out," said Sara.

"Yes," said Mrs. Kendrick. "Ever since Adam sinned, we have all been born wanting to sin. The Bible says that we go the wrong way as soon as we're born. And then when things go wrong, we often blame others.

"When God talked to Adam after he had sinned, Adam said, 'The woman you gave me, she gave me the fruit and I ate it.' Then Eve said, 'The serpent tempted me and I ate it.' Each one blamed someone else. But they were both guilty, weren't they? Often we, too, try to blame something or someone for our sin, but each of us is guilty of it. The Bible says, 'All have sinned and

fall short of the glory of God.'

"Whether we have sinned greatly or very little," Mrs. Kendrick went on, "each of us has broken God's law. Only those who have trusted Christ to save them have had their guilt removed. Some day Kay will understand this."

"Kay didn't break the vase," Kay said emphatically. And everyone looked at each other and smiled.

TO DISCUSS

Do small children disobey their parents and tell lies? Does someone teach them to do wrong? If not, why do they do wrong? Have you sinned?

TO DO

Fill in the missing words from Romans 3:23.
For _____ have sinned and _____ short of the _____ of God.
For all have _____ and fall _____ of the glory of _____.
For _____ have _____ and _____ _____ of the _____
of _____.

TO PRAY

If you're a sinner, would you like to ask Jesus to forgive your sins and save you? If you're a Christian, do you have some sin in your life you need to confess to God?

CHAPTER THIRTY-FOUR

Sin's Payday

Romans 6:23

For the wages of sin is death, but the gift of God is eternal life in Christ Jesus our Lord. NKJV

James 1:14-15

Temptation is the pull of man's own evil thoughts and wishes. These evil thoughts lead to evil actions and afterwards to the death penalty from God. TLB

One day Mike showed Joshua a present his uncle had given him. "It's an Australian boomerang," he said. "The native Australians use it to kill birds and small animals. When they throw it, if it misses its target, it curves in the air and returns to the thrower, close enough for him to catch it."

"That's neat," said Joshua. "Let's go outside and see if we can make it come back."

On his first throw, Mike landed the boomerang in the bushes. But after some practice, both boys could get the boomerang to return most of the time.

At the next Bible Explorers meeting, the boys demonstrated their new skill to Mrs. Kendrick and the girls. Then, as the lesson began, Mrs. Kendrick said, "Mike, your boomerang is a good illustration of today's lesson, called 'Sin's Payday.' Sin is something like a boomerang. It starts with you, and it comes back to you, bringing its penalty. When Adam and Eve sinned, they had to suffer the consequences. What was the penalty God promised they'd have if they sinned?"

"He said they would die," answered Sara. "But they didn't die right away, did they? Adam lived to be very, very old."

"You need to understand what the word *death* means," said Mrs. Kendrick. It never means 'to stop.' It means 'separation.'

"There are three kinds of death. The first is *spiritual death.* A sinner is separated from God by his sin.

Spiritual death happened to Adam and Eve right away when they sinned. Another death is *physical death.* When a person's body dies, it separates from his soul and spirit, which live on. After many years, Adam and Eve died physically. The final death is *eternal death.* On Judgment Day, all sinners, because they haven't received Jesus as Savior, will be separated from God forever in the lake of fire."

"Will Adam and Eve go there?" asked Mike.

"Evidently, Adam and Eve believed God would forgive them when they sinned. I expect to see them in heaven one day."

TO DISCUSS

What does *death* mean? What are the three kinds of death? What happens when you trust Jesus as your Savior?

TO DO

Draw a line down a sheet of paper. On one side draw something that reminds you of death (a cross, a tombstone, etc.). On the other side draw something that reminds you of the gift of eternal life (a pretty package, beautiful flowers, etc.). At the bottom of your paper, copy the words of Romans 6:23: "For the wages of sin is death, but the gift of God is eternal life in Christ Jesus our Lord."

TO PRAY

Thank the Lord Jesus that he died on the cross so that you wouldn't have to have eternal death someday. If you have never received Jesus as your Savior, would you like to do so now?

CHAPTER THIRTY-FIVE

When a Christian Sins

Psalm 32:1-5

What happiness for those whose guilt has been forgiven! What joys when sins are covered over! What relief for those who have confessed their sins and God has cleared their record.

There was a time when I wouldn't admit what a sinner I was. But my dishonesty made me miserable and filled my days with frustration . . . until I finally admitted all my sins to you and stopped trying to hide them. I said to myself, "I will confess them to the Lord." And you forgave me! All my guilt is gone. TLB

1 John 1:9

If we confess our sins, He is faithful and just to forgive us our sins and to cleanse us from all unrighteousness. NKJV

Catch it, Ranger!" called out Mike, sailing a Frisbee into the air. Ranger raced to catch the disk, with Mike close behind. Mike didn't notice his mother's pansy bed until he had stepped into it, crushing several plants.

Uh-oh! Mike thought. *Mom's prize pansies! I don't want her to know about this.* Pulling up the ruined plants, he dumped them into the garbage can.

That night, when Mike didn't mention the plants, his older sister Karen said, "I saw you in the pansy bed. I won't tell Mom if you'll do all my chores this week." So after doing his own chores, Mike offered to take out the garbage for Karen. The next morning he washed the dishes in her place. At dinner, though, he refused to set the table for her. With a sly smile, she whispered, "Squashed pansies." Mike made a face, but he set the table.

On the fourth day, Mike told Karen to wash the dishes herself. "I'm not doing your chores anymore," he said.

"Squashed pansies!" Karen said. "I'll tell!"

"Go ahead; I don't care," said Mike. "I was tired of hearing 'squashed pansies,' so last night I told Mom what I did. I said I was sorry, and she forgave me. Now you do your own chores, Karen. I'm free!"

At the next Bible Explorers meeting, Mrs. Kendrick said, "Our recent lessons have been about sin. We have learned that sin brings troubles to people. Even after we're saved, sometimes we sin. Do Christians have any troubles because of sinning?"

"I know one thing that happens," said Mike. "You feel real guilty inside." He told the others about the squashed pansies.

"When I told Mom, she forgave me, and I felt a lot better. And Karen couldn't accuse me anymore."

"Something like that happened to David when he sinned so terribly," Mrs. Kendrick said. "He said he felt like he'd had a roaring inside him all day long. That is, his feeling of guilt was like a lion in a cage, roaring to get out. But when he confessed his sin, God forgave him, and he was free from guilt.

"The Holy Spirit convicts us of sin and urges us to confess it. He won't allow us to have peace or joy until we do. But isn't our heavenly Father merciful? When we confess our sins, the blood of Jesus cleanses us, and we are free from all guilt."

Mike grinned. "It sure is good to be free!" he said.

TO DISCUSS

If you disobey your parents, do they kick you out of the family? Even if they said you no longer were their child, would that be so? Why not? Could God's child get unborn? Do your parents discipline you for disobeying? Does God? What should you do as soon as you know you have sinned? What will God do when you tell him you are sorry?

TO DO

Cross out every other word in the following sentence, and then read it aloud: "If sin we sin confess sin our sin sins, sin He sin is sin faithful sin and sin just sin to sin forgive sin us sin our sin sins sin and sin to sin cleanse sin us sin from sin all sin unrighteousness sin" (1 John 1:9). Aren't you glad God removes every one of your sins when you confess them to him?

TO PRAY

If you are a Christian with some unconfessed sin in your life, would you confess it to God now? Thank him for forgiving your sins and cleansing you.

PART **8**

Jesus Saves Us

Acts 4:12

Nor is there salvation in any other, for there
is no other name under heaven given
among men by which we must be saved. *NKJV*

▶ ▶ ▶

CHAPTER THIRTY-SIX

1 Peter 3:18
Christ also suffered. He died once for the sins of all us guilty sinners although he himself was innocent of any sin at any time, that he might bring us safely home to God. TLB

Jesus Took Your Punishment

At the next Bible Explorers meeting, Mike said, "Mrs. Kendrick, sometimes my folks will listen now when I tell them about Jesus. They say I sure act different since I asked him to save me. But Dad said, 'Your mom and I have sinned too much. God would never take us to heaven.' What can I tell him?"

"None of us deserve heaven," said Mrs. Kendrick, "whether our sins are very great or very little. Talk to your parents about this, Mike, and then tell them this story about two boys who lived in Scotland long ago:

"These boys were great friends as they grew up. But later their paths separated. One day they met again in a courtroom. One of them was a judge, and the other was a condemned criminal,

JESUS SAVES US

brought before the judge for sentencing. The criminal recognized the judge. *Oh,* he thought, *he is my long-ago playmate. Surely he will go easy on me.* Turning to the judge, he said, 'Sir, do you recognize me?'

"'Yes, I do,' replied the judge. 'I have studied your case and the penalties that the law books say I should give.'

"'Oh, please, sir, for the sake of our old friendship, give me a small penalty,' pleaded the criminal. The judge, however, ordered that he should pay a sum of money that was so large the man could never pay it and would have to go to prison. The criminal bowed his head, and tears slipped down his cheeks.

"'George, George, my old friend,' said the judge. 'I have judged you as a just judge, but now I will save you as a friend. I indeed fixed a great penalty, but I will now pay the whole amount myself. You are a free man.'

"Boys and girls," Mrs. Kendrick went on, "God is the Judge of all the world. He set the penalty for sin— eternal death in hell. He has to

punish sin because he can't set aside his law. But God loved us so much that he gave his Son to take our punishment. Jesus didn't deserve to die, did he? He never sinned. But he took our place because he loves us so much. He let cruel men nail him to a cross, where he shed his blood and died. Now he's alive. He wants us to believe in him and ask him to forgive our sins. When we do, we are free from all punishment."

"I'm going to tell this story to my parents," said Mike.

"Let's all keep praying that they will listen to and trust Jesus," said Joshua. And everyone agreed.

TO DISCUSS

Who is guilty of sin? What is the punishment that God has set for sinners? Who is the only one who has never sinned? When he died on the cross, whose punishment did he take? Who can go free from punishment?

TO DO

On a piece of paper, draw a stick figure hanging on a cross. Underneath it write, "Jesus never sinned. He took my punishment. When I believe in him, I go free from punishment."

TO PRAY

Thank Jesus for taking your punishment by dying for you on the cross.

Change Your Mind and Turn from Sin

Matthew 7:13-14
Enter through the narrow gate. For wide is the gate and broad is the road that leads to destruction, and many enter through it. But small is the gate and narrow the road that leads to life, and only a few find it. NIV

John 14:6
Jesus said to him, "I am the way, the truth, and the life. No one comes to the Father except through Me." NKJV

"Dad, are we getting near Hampton?" asked Joshua. "The game starts in less than an hour."

Dad looked at the odometer. "We've come twelve miles since we stopped for gas," he said, "so we have about ten miles more. You'll have plenty of time to get into your uniforms."

Joshua and Mike sat back impatiently. Then Joshua said, "Dad, I think we were on this road before. Everything looks familiar. Maybe we got on the wrong road at the gas station."

"I'm sure we didn't," said Dad. But soon he blurted out, "Oh no! That sign says Jonesville is ahead.

We're not supposed to go there. I did make a wrong turn after getting gas."

Joshua groaned. "Turn around fast, Dad," he begged.

"We can't turn around on the interstate," Dad replied. "We'll have to wait for a crossover road."

Riding along for several more miles, the boys watched the traffic on the other side of the highway. "There they go—headed the way we want to go, but can't," moaned Mike. At last, though, they reached an exit, crossed over, and continued traveling toward Hampton. They arrived a few minutes late, but the coach let the boys suit up and get into the game.

Telling of their experience at the next Bible Explorers meeting, Mike said, "I'm sure glad we found a crossover road when we did."

Mrs. Kendrick turned to Matthew 7:13-14. "Here Jesus speaks of two ways," she said. "They are the narrow road to heaven and the broad road that leads to hell. He urged us to get on the road to heaven. But in order to do that, we must go by the only 'crossover road,' and that is Jesus. He is the way to heaven."

"I guess a lot of folks are like us,"

said Joshua. "They don't realize they're going the wrong way. Even when I told Dad I thought we were headed in the wrong direction, he didn't believe it at first."

"Our lesson today is about repentance," said Mrs. Kendrick. "To repent is to turn away from sin. A sinner must realize he is going away from God, not toward him. He must be sorry for his sin and turn from it.

When he does so, believing that Jesus died for his sins, God places his feet on the narrow way that leads to heaven. By the way of the cross, he has turned from the broad way and entered the narrow way."

"I'm glad we found a crossover road on the interstate," said Mike, "and I'm glad sinners can cross to the narrow way. Best of all, I'm glad I did that."

TO DISCUSS

Are you allowed to cross over to the other side of an interstate road at just any point along the way? What must you wait for? How do we get from the road to hell to the road to heaven? The only way to heaven is a person. Who is he? What did he do to become our way? What is repentance?

TO DO

On your notebook page, draw a fire (hell) in the bottom left-hand corner. Draw a broad road across the bottom of the page, leading to it. At the top, in the far right-hand corner, draw a picture representing heaven. Draw a narrow road across the top of your paper, leading to it. Between the two roads, draw a cross. Beside it write, "Jesus is the way to heaven."

TO PRAY

Thank Jesus that he died on the cross and rose again so that you might get on the only road to heaven.

CHAPTER THIRTY-EIGHT

Believe Jesus Will Save You

Luke 4:16-19

He went to Nazareth, where he had been brought up, and on the Sabbath day he went into the synagogue, as was his custom. And he stood up to read. The scroll of the prophet Isaiah was handed to him. Unrolling it, he found the place where it is written:

"The Spirit of the Lord is on me, because he has anointed me to preach good news to the poor. He has sent me to proclaim freedom for the prisoners and recovery of sight for the blind, to release the oppressed, to proclaim the year of the Lord's favor." NIV

John 8:36

Therefore if the Son makes you free, you shall be free indeed. NKJV

A prison was located not far from the town where the Bible Explorers lived. One time an inmate planned a daring escape. Night after night, while others were asleep, he sawed on the metal bars of his window, using a metal spoon, which he had sharpened. Finally, the bars were nearly cut through.

The next night he finished the job and pulled the bars away. Then he tied some sheets together. Fastening one end to his bed, he let the other end down through the window. Then he crawled through the window and slid down to the ground on the sheets. To his great surprise, a guard was waiting for him there with a gun. "We've been watching you," he said. "Now you will go to a federal prison where no one has ever escaped."

The prisoner's story was in the newspaper, and the Bible Explorers talked about it at their next meeting. "He sure did a lot of work for nothing, didn't he?" said Mike.

"Did you know that sinners are in a prison that they can't break out of?" asked Mrs. Kendrick. "It's a spiritual prison—the prison of sin. Many sinners try to escape from it by doing good works, going to church, trusting a false religion, or something similar. No matter what they do, though, they can't escape from their prison by themselves."

"Jesus can take them out, can't he?" asked Jodie.

"That's right," said Mrs. Kendrick. "One time, in a synagogue at Nazareth, Jesus told his listeners that he had come to deliver the captives—those who were in the prison of sin. He made this possible when he died on the cross and rose again.

"In our last lesson, we talked about repentance—turning from sin. Once we turn from sin (repentance) we must also turn toward God. When we believe in God, we call that faith. Repentance and faith are like two

sides of the same coin—you can't have one without the other.

"When each of you repented and believed, God removed you from the prison of sin and placed you in his family. Jesus washed away every sin. You were made so clean that, in God's sight, it was as though you had never been in the prison of sin at all."

TO DISCUSS

What are some ways by which people try to break out of the prison of sin? Which of these will work? Who can break them out of the prison of sin?

TO DO

Place a quarter underneath a piece of paper and rub across it with a pencil, transferring the markings to your page. Turn the coin over, and do the same with the other side. Underneath one write, "Repentance," and underneath the other write, "Faith." At the bottom write, "One salvation. Two sides."

TO PRAY

Read Psalm 142:7. Thank Jesus that he died on the cross to bring us out of the prison of sin.

Can You Be Sure of Heaven?

John 5:24
I tell you the truth, whoever hears my word and believes him who sent me has eternal life and will not be condemned; he has crossed over from death to life. NIV

1 John 5:13
These things I have written to you who believe in the name of the Son of God, that you may know that you have eternal life. NKJV

One Saturday morning, the Murphys took the Bible Explorers, along with Mr. and Mrs. Kendrick, to a large lake. "Across the lake is a nice beach," Mr. Murphy said. "We'll go over there in our boat for a swim and a picnic."

Everyone put on life jackets and boarded the boat. With Mr. Murphy at the wheel, they headed for the other side. Pretty soon Mrs. Kendrick noticed that while the other children were moving about the boat, laughing and having a good time, Sara sat with her back against a cabin wall, looking unhappy.

"What's wrong, Sara?" Mrs. Kendrick asked. "Are you sick?"

Sara shook her head. "No, Aunt Betty," she said. "I'm scared. The rest of you are used to the water, but I'm not. I can't even swim. What if the boat goes down? I'd drown."

Mrs. Kendrick sat down by her niece and put her arms around her. "You have on a life jacket, honey," she said. "I'm sure this boat will make it to land safely. But if it did sink, you would float with that life jacket until you were rescued. You aren't helping anything by sitting here. Why don't you go ahead and play with the other children?"

Sara managed a little smile and stood up. "OK," she said. "I'll try to enjoy the trip."

After their picnic, Mrs. Kendrick talked about Sara's fears. "You know," she said, "Sara was just as safe as the rest of you on the boat, but she wasn't enjoying herself. She's like Christians who have trusted Christ but aren't really enjoying the trip to heaven because they're afraid they might lose their salvation. Jesus wants us to have joy and peace in our hearts. What are some ways that we can know we'll make it to heaven?"

"Well, Jesus said that if we believe in him, we'll have everlasting life," said Joshua. "That's forever—not getting halfway to heaven and losing salvation."

"Yeah, and John 3:16 says that whoever believes in Jesus will never perish," added Sara.

"And when I read the Bible and pray, God speaks to me in my heart," said Mike. "And I like to tell others about him."

"He sure does," said Mr. Murphy. "Mike's been telling us about your Bible lessons on salvation." He paused. Then he went on. "The main reason I planned this trip was so my wife and I could talk with you. We want to make sure of heaven. Would you help us?" The Bible Explorers looked at one another and smiled. It was what they had been praying for!

On the return trip, everyone felt safe and secure, even Sara. Not only were they headed for land, they were all on their way to heaven, too.

TO DISCUSS

In the story, how many made it safely to land? How many felt unsafe? Was Sara just as safe as the others? What kind of life does the Bible say believers have? How long does that last? Has Satan ever caused you to doubt your salvation? What can you tell him the next time he wants you to doubt?

TO DO

Solve the puzzle "What Kind of Life Does Jesus Give?"

TO PRAY

Thank the Lord for the Bible, which tells us we can be sure of salvation. If you have trusted Jesus as your Savior, thank him that he has given you everlasting life.

What Kind of Life Does Jesus Give?

Fill in the blanks by adding or subtracting the letters of the alphabet to find the letters needed. What verse in the Bible do these words remind you of?

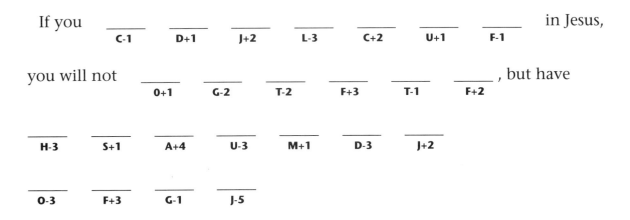

If you _____ _____ _____ _____ _____ _____ _____ in Jesus,
C-1   D+1   J+2   L-3   C+2   U+1   F-1

you will not _____ _____ _____ _____ _____ _____ , but have
O+1   G-2   T-2   F+3   T-1   F+2

_____ _____ _____ _____ _____ _____ _____
H-3   S+1   A+4   U-3   M+1   D-3   J+2

_____ _____ _____ _____
O-3   F+3   G-1   J-5

A B C D E F G H I J K L M N O P Q R S T U V W X Y Z

Answer is on page 230.

CHAPTER FORTY

Romans 12:1-2

I beseech you therefore, brethren, by the mercies of God, that you present your bodies a living sacrifice, holy, acceptable to God, which is your reasonable service. And do not be conformed to this world, but be transformed by the renewing of your mind, that you may prove what is that good and acceptable and perfect will of God. NKJV

Set Apart for God

When the Bible Explorers met again, Joshua, instead of greeting the others, just sat in a corner, looking glum. "Hey, what's the matter?" asked Mike. "Are you sick?"

Joshua shook his head, "No," he replied. "I just found out my whole life is ruined. Dad and Mom told me this morning that we're going to be missionaries to an Indian tribe in Brazil. I'll have to live in the jungle! I won't have any friends, and I'll never be able to play baseball again."

"I think I understand how you feel, Son," his mother said. "After all, my life will be greatly changed, too. But God has called us, and we must go."

"Well, God didn't call me, but I have to go, too," Joshua retorted. "I guess God doesn't care what happens to me."

"Oh, but he does care," his mom assured him. "God knew you'd have to go; so this move will be best for you, too." Joshua frowned. This was best for him? No way!

"Our study of the plan of salvation isn't quite finished," Mrs. Kendrick said to the Bible Explorers. "There is a big word that I want to explain to you. It is *sanctification.* It means 'to be set apart.' Believers are set apart in three ways. First, when we are saved, we are set apart from the devil's family and belong to God's family. Second, we should let God set us apart to live for him day by day. Third, someday, when we get to heaven, we will be set apart from sin, pain, and troubles forever.

"It is that second part that we ourselves must do something about—being set apart to live for God. Three persons want to rule your life: Jesus, Satan, and yourself. Who should rule?"

"Jesus," answered all the Bible Explorers at once.

"Why should he?" asked Mrs. Kendrick.

"Because he died for us," answered Jodie.

"Yes," said Mrs. Kendrick. "Jesus has the right to rule, doesn't he? Also, he knows what is best for us. He is gentle and kind. He loves us and wants us to be happy. But sometimes we want to run our own lives. We don't want to do what Jesus says. That is when Satan can easily tempt us to do wrong, and he begins to run our life. He never wants what is best for us.

"Bible Explorers, God wants you to give him your life to do what he wants to with it," Mrs. Kendrick continued. "From then on, when you awake on each new day, ask him to take charge of you and, with the Holy Spirit's help, to keep you from sin. If Jesus loved you enough to die for you, don't you think you can trust him with your life? Who would like to kneel in prayer now, asking Jesus to be your King and run your life from now on?"

Mike, Sara, and Jodie knelt by their chairs. After a brief pause, Joshua did, too. Later, wiping the tears from his eyes, he said, "I know I can trust Jesus to do the best thing for me. Maybe going to Brazil won't be so bad after all. It could be the greatest adventure of my life!"

TO DISCUSS

Are you afraid to let God have his way in your life? Do you think that obeying him will make you unhappy and miserable? Doing what God wants may not mean you'll be a missionary. Can you think of other ways that God may direct your life? If Jesus loved you enough to die for you, would he want to hurt you and make you unhappy when you do what he wants?

TO DO

If you truly love Jesus and want him to run your life, write a letter to him on a piece of paper, and tell him that.

TO PRAY

Thank Jesus that he knows what's best for you. Ask him to be your King from now on.

PART 9

Doing God's Will

Galatians 2:20

I have been crucified with Christ and I no longer live, but Christ lives in me. The life I live in the body, I live by faith in the Son of God, who loved me and gave himself for me.

CHAPTER FORTY-ONE

1 Corinthians 14:15
So what shall I do? I will pray with my spirit, but I will also pray with my mind; I will sing with my spirit, but I will also sing with my mind.
NIV

Worship God at Church

I liked hearing the missionary at our children's church yesterday, didn't you?" Mike asked the other Bible Explorers at a club meeting. "Mrs. Kendrick, he told us about some people who worship a false god. It is a fifty-foot Buddha that sits outside a temple. Inside are one thousand of the Buddha's friends, lined up along two walls. The people walk along the wall, bowing before all the idols. Then they go outside and bow again and again before the Buddha. They think that their god will give them honor, long life, and good luck when they worship him like that."

"I'm glad we know better than that," said Joshua. "That idol can't hear or see those people. When we go to church, we worship the true God."

"What do you like best about going to church?" asked Mrs. Kendrick.

"I like to sing the songs," said Sara. "They make me feel happy."

"I like to hear Bible lessons and preaching," said Mike.

"I think about God more at church," said Joshua.

"I like being with other Christians," said Jodie.

"All of these are excellent reasons for going to church," said Mrs. Kendrick. "God wants us to attend, and he warns us not to stay away from his house."

"But can't we worship him other places?" asked Sara. "God is in all places."

"That's true," said Mrs. Kendrick. "Wherever we are, we should remember that God is there, too. We can talk to him at any moment. But at church we don't have other things to take our mind away from God. When we meet with other Christians, we think about him as we sing, pray, and study the Bible."

"My trouble is, sometimes I just do those things and don't really think about God," admitted Joshua.

"I know what you mean," said his mother. "I've caught myself thinking about what I'll fix for dinner, or something like that, while singing the old, familiar hymns. We should always keep our mind on God and his Word at church. If we don't, I guess we're not worshiping God any more than people who bow to idols. Shall we all promise God that, with his help, we'll try to truly worship him at church from now on?"

TO DISCUSS

What are you thinking about when the songs are being sung at church? When someone prays, do you pray, too? When the sermon is preached, what could you do to try to understand it better? What kind of promise would you like to make to God about worshiping him at church?

TO DO

On a piece of paper, write these words, leaving blanks to fill in beside each one:
1. Songs we sang.
2. The Scripture that was read (just the references).
3. One thought from the sermon.

When you come home from your next church service, see if you can fill in all the blanks. (You may write brief notes at church to remind you if you wish.) Do this for the next several services, and see if it won't help you pay better attention and worship God better.

TO PRAY

Ask the Lord to help you really worship him at church.

CHAPTER FORTY-TWO

Be a Shining Witness for God

Ephesians 5:8-14

For though once your heart was full of darkness, now it is full of light from the Lord, and your behavior should show it! Because of this light within you, you should do only what is good and right and true.

Learn as you go along what pleases the Lord. Take no part in the worthless pleasures of evil and darkness, but instead, rebuke and expose them. . . . When you expose them, the light shines in upon their sin and shows it up, and when they see how wrong they really are, some of them may even become children of light! That is why God says in the Scriptures, "Awake, O sleeper, and rise up from the dead; and Christ shall give you light."
TLB

Hey, Mom, guess what?" Sara said, walking into her mother's room. "Jodie just phoned, and she wants me to spend the day with her and her mom at the mall. They're leaving soon. Please, may I go?"

"Yes, if you can clean your room in time," her mom answered. "Pick up your things and vacuum the floor. And clean your windows, too. They're very dirty."

Sara hurried to phone her friend. "Mom says I may go after I clean my room," she informed her. "I'll do that in no time."

When Sara looked at her room, though, she wasn't so sure. What a mess! Her things were strewn everywhere. But the windows looked fine. "I'll just give them a quick swipe with a paper towel," she said to herself. "And I'll stuff

185

everything that's out of place into the back of my closet. When I come home, I'll put it all away." She raced around the room and soon ran to tell her mother, "Come see my room, Mom. It's clean."

As she and her mother walked into her room, Sara gasped. The sun had come out and was shining directly through her windowpanes. The dirt that she hadn't seen before was plainly visible now, and there were streaks across it where she had wiped with the paper towel. "Oh, Mom," she wailed, "look at the dirt! I didn't see it before, so I thought I'd get by without much cleaning." Then, with a sheepish smile, she added, "The sunshine showed me up, didn't it?"

Sara told the other Bible Explorers about her windows the next day. "That's a good example of what Jesus, the Light of the World, does in our lives," Mrs. Kendrick said. "We may

think our lives are spotlessly clean; but if we will examine them in the light of his Word and his perfect example, we'll often see sins that need to be cleansed away. That's why we must shine his light into every dark corner of our lives.

"Jesus is the Light of the World," Mrs. Kendrick went on. "He is not here in bodily form now, but he is inside believers. We are to be lights to the world by letting Jesus shine through us, so that others may see our good works and praise God."

"You know, yesterday I had to get a good cleaner and work on my windows," said Sara. "Now I think I need to ask Jesus to clean me from my sin of lying to Mom about my room."

TO DISCUSS

Do you think most sinners read the Bible? If they don't, how are they going to learn about Jesus? What will sinners pay the most attention to—what you say or what you do?

TO DO

On a piece of paper, draw a white heart with a shining sun inside. Underneath write, "Jesus, the Light of the World, shines in a Christian's heart." Draw another identical heart, with dark streaks across it. Write underneath it, "Sin will hide Jesus so sinners can't see him."

TO PRAY

Ask Jesus to help you be a witness for him today, both with your words and your actions.

CHAPTER FORTY-THREE

Psalm 119:16

I delight in your decrees; I will not neglect your word. NIV

Psalm 119:72

The law from your mouth is more precious to me than thousands of pieces of silver and gold. NIV

1 Thessalonians 5:17

Pray without ceasing. NKJV

Study the Bible and Pray

One day Mrs. Kendrick told the Bible Explorers two true stories. Would you like to hear them?

Their Own Bibles

Prema and Jaya sat under a big tree and watched the other children at play. Prema (whose name means "love") and her brother, Jaya ("victory"), were orphan children who lived at a mission boarding school at Kavali, South India. "Prema, don't you wish you had a Bible?" asked Jaya. "I do. Since I received Jesus as my Savior, I want to read it every day. But it's hard to borrow one all the time."

"Yes, and we are too poor to buy Bibles," replied Prema.

Just then a boy walked by with a basket, headed

for the bungalow where the missionary, Miss Ruth, lived. "That's it!" exclaimed Jaya. "Misamma Ruth will give us a Bible for bringing her baskets of buffalo chips [dried manure from buffaloes]. They are used for fertilizer."

"We could do that!" said Prema, her eyes sparkling. At once Prema and Jaya began hunting for chips. When their baskets were filled to the top, they brought them to Miss Ruth.

"Do you want to earn Bibles, too?" Miss Ruth asked them.

"Yes, Misamma," they replied.

"You each have nineteen more to go, then," she said, as she recorded their names and the amount they brought.

Day by day the children filled their baskets with chips. At last they heard the good news—they each had only one more basket to fill! The next day, Prema and Jaya proudly brought their filled baskets to Miss Ruth and eagerly held out their hands to receive their new Telugu Bibles.

"My very own Bible!" cried Prema, hugging it close.

"It was worth all the hard, smelly work, wasn't it?" said Jaya with a big smile. "Now we can read God's Word every day!"

Bruised for Praying to Jesus

Kim received Jesus as her Savior at a mission school. A few days later, she came to school with terrible bruises on her forehead. "What happened to you?" the missionary asked.

"I know," another child spoke up. "Her father asked her why she would not bow and pray to their idol. She said she prays to Jesus, the true God, now. He took her to their idol and hit her head down very hard on the stones in front of it. She bled a whole lot. Kim cried and cried."

"Never mind," said Kim. "Idols made out of wood and stone cannot hear my prayers, but Jesus can. He loves me, and he listens to me when I pray."

After the stories, Mrs. Kendrick said, "Bible Explorers, you each have a Bible. No one will hurt you for praying to God. It is very important for you to read the Bible and pray. Do you appreciate how easy it is for you to do those things? Are you careful to do them every day?"

TO DISCUSS

Do you think Prema and Jaya neglected their Bible after working so hard to get it? Did you have to pick up twenty baskets of buffalo chips to get your Bible? Has anyone ever made you bow before an idol? Do you read your Bible? Do you pray?

TO DO

On a piece of paper draw a picture of your favorite food. Beside it, draw a Bible. Beneath them, write, "My body needs food to grow. My soul needs God's Word to grow." Beside it, draw some praying hands. Beneath them, write, "My body needs air to live. My soul needs prayer to live the Christian life."

TO PRAY

Thank Jesus for your Bible and for the privilege of talking to him at any time. Will you try very hard to read the Bible and pray every day?

CHAPTER FORTY-FOUR

Colossians 3:20

Children, obey your parents in all things, for this is well pleasing to the Lord. NKJV

Obey Your Parents

Joshua and his dad were headed home from a trip. As they passed through a town, a red light flashed on the dashboard panel. "That's the alternator's warning light," said Dad. "Maybe I should stop, but I think we'll make it home all right."

When they were miles from any houses, the car lights grew very dim. "Uh-oh, I think I made a bad mistake," said Dad. The engine sputtered and stopped, and Dad steered the car to the side of the road.

First, Joshua and Dad bowed their heads and asked God to protect them and send somebody to help. Then Dad put up the hood to show that they needed help. Car after car sped by, and no one stopped. At last a sheriff's deputy arrived and called for a tow truck to come.

As they waited, Dad said, "Look at the trouble I've caused by not paying attention to that warning light! If I had stopped when it flashed, I would have saved us money, time, and a possibly dangerous situation."

At Bible Explorers Club, Mrs. Kendrick told the children about what had happened. "It was very foolish of my husband not to pay attention to the warning light," she said. "It was very dangerous for them to be out on that dark highway late at night.

"Did you know, Bible Explorers, that God gave you your mom and dad to be something like that light? You see, your parents have lived a lot longer than you have. They have learned much from experience and from reading the Bible and good books. So they know much more than you do about life. It is for your own good that they warn you not to do something."

"But sometimes we don't pay attention," said Joshua. "Then we get in trouble, just like Dad and I did when he didn't pay attention to the warning light."

"Have you ever thought that your folks were too hard on you when they refused to let you do something?" Mrs. Kendrick asked. One by one, all the children nodded their heads. "Your parents love you," Mrs. Kendrick went on. "They aren't trying to be mean when they make rules or when they discipline you."

"If our folks didn't discipline us

when we do wrong, I guess that would show they didn't care what happens to us," said Sara.

Mrs. Kendrick smiled. "Don't ever forget that, Sara," she said. "No one likes to be punished. But the more you learn now about obedience, the less trouble you will get into later in life. You see, when you learn to obey your parents and teachers, you will be better citizens, obeying the laws of the land. Best of all, you will learn to obey God."

TO DISCUSS

If a smoke alarm goes off at your house, and you hear it but stay in bed, what might happen to you? If you walk when there is a Don't Walk sign, what might happen? Why do your parents tell you to do some things and not to do others? If you don't pay attention to their warnings, what kind of person might you turn out to be? If your parents discipline you, does that mean they don't love you?

TO DO

Copy the words of Colossians 3:20 on a piece of paper. Underline with red the word that tells you in how many things you are to obey.

TO PRAY

Thank the Lord for your parents. Ask him to help you obey them in everything.

CHAPTER FORTY-FIVE

Say No to Sin

1 Peter 3:13-17

Usually no one will hurt you for wanting to do good. But even if they should, you are to be envied, for God will reward you for it. Quietly trust yourself to Christ your Lord, and if anybody asks why you believe as you do, be ready to tell him, and do it in a gentle and respectful way.

Do what is right; then if men speak against you, calling you evil names, they will become ashamed of themselves for falsely accusing you when you have only done what is good. Remember, if God wants you to suffer, it is better to suffer for doing good than for doing wrong! TLB

Jodie, hoping to join in a game, walked over to a large ring of children in the school yard. "Hi, Jodie," said Lisa. "You can play if you have some nickels to toss into the circle. Whoever gets the most inside may keep all the nickels."

Jodie shook her head. "No, I don't have any nickels," she said. "I'll just watch."

"Be sure to bring some nickels tomorrow," Lisa insisted. "With more nickels, the winner's prize will be bigger."

At Bible Explorers Club, Jodie told Mrs. Kendrick about the game. "Isn't that sort of like gambling?" she asked.

"Yes, it is," said Mrs. Kendrick. "I'm glad you chose not to play."

"Yeah, but now I don't know what to do," said Jodie with a sigh. "Since my folks put me in this private school, I haven't made any friends. If I don't play the games the other kids want to play and do what they tell me, I'm afraid they won't like me. What can I do?"

"You need to tell the other children why you won't join in certain activities. Tell them right away that you're a Christian," Mrs. Kendrick told her. "It won't get easier if you wait. It will get harder."

"But what if they make fun of me?" asked Jodie. "I'm a new Christian, and I'm real shy. I'd never deny Jesus, but I wish I didn't have to tell the kids for a while that I'm a Christian."

Mrs. Kendrick walked to the kitchen and returned with some boxes of cereal. "Children," she said, "I want you to notice the front of these boxes. Each one very prominently displays

the name of the company that sells the cereal. Do you suppose they believe what they're offering to the public is good and wholesome?"

"They sure must!" replied Mike with a grin. "They advertise it on TV."

"Then having their name on the outside puts their stamp of approval on the product inside, doesn't it?" Mrs. Kendrick asked.

"Sure," said Sara, and the others agreed.

"The Lord Jesus lives inside you,

boys and girls," Mrs. Kendrick said. "He is the King of kings. Your friends need him. Don't be ashamed to advertise him. One of the best ways to do that is to say no when they ask you to join them in some sin. When they ask you why, tell them that you're a Christian."

"Sometimes they call me chicken when I don't do what they do," said

Mike. "That sure makes a guy feel stupid."

"You won't feel that way if you remember who's inside of you," said Mrs. Kendrick. "Next time say, 'No, I'm not a chicken, I'm a Christian, and I'm proud to say I have Jesus, the King of kings inside of me. Wouldn't you like to have him, too?'"

TO DISCUSS

Do others know that Jesus is inside you? Do you refuse to go along with the crowd when they do wrong? Do you kneel to pray before going to bed at a friend's home? Do you pray before eating your school lunch? Put your "stamp of approval" on Jesus by proudly declaring that he's inside you.

TO DO

On a piece of paper, copy the words of the rebus puzzle "I Can Say No," using words instead of the pictures.

TO PRAY

Ask Jesus to help you proudly advertise him today.

I Can Say No

I'm not a [duck] or a [ ]. I'm a Christian who has [Jesus] in my [heart]. He is the [king] of kings. If a [girl] or a [boy] asks me to do wrong, I will say NO and proudly tell [woman] [girl] [boy] [man] that I [love] [Jesus].

Answer is on page 231.

PART 10

Becoming like Jesus

Romans 12:1-2

I beseech you therefore, brethren, by the mercies of God, that you present your bodies a living sacrifice, holy, acceptable to God, which is your reasonable service. And do not be conformed to this world, but be transformed by the renewing of your mind, that you may prove what is that good and acceptable and perfect will of God. *NKJV*

▶ ▶ ▶

CHAPTER FORTY-SIX

Colossians 3:23-24
Whatever you do, work at it with all your heart, as working for the Lord, not for men. NIV

Develop Your Talents

Plink! Plink! Plink! One by one Sara slowly picked out the notes of her new piano recital piece. "This piece is too hard, Mom," she said. "I'll never get it." She struggled on for a few minutes—*plink, plink, plink.* Suddenly she slammed the music book shut and began to play some of the music she knew from memory. Oh, this was much more fun!

"Sara, I'm going to plant some seeds in my flower garden," Mom said. "Come along for a few minutes."

Sara followed her mom to the backyard. "You had the most beautiful flowers in our neighborhood in Kansas, Mom," she said. "Grandma says you have a green thumb—whatever that means."

Mom laughed. "She means I have a talent for growing things. That may be true, but I have to put in a lot of hard work, too. Thomas Edison, the great inventor, said, 'Genius is one percent inspiration and 99 percent perspiration.'" Mom held one of the seeds in her hand. "Look at this, Sara. Do you know what this hard little thing is? It's a possibility. Just think what it can become one day!"

Sara looked at the seed thoughtfully. "It's hard to imagine that it will become a living plant with green leaves and pretty flowers," she said.

"Would it ever become a plant if I just left it in the seed packet?" Mom asked.

"Oh no. You have to hoe the ground and plant the seed. Then you must give it water and fertilizer," Sara replied.

As Mom began to drop some seeds into the soil, she asked, "You plan to be a good pianist someday, don't you?"

Sara smiled. "Oh yes," she said enthusiastically. "I hope to be a very good pianist."

"God has given you the talent to become one," Mom said. "But, like the little seed, right now your talent

is only a possibility. If you want to develop it into something great and worthwhile, you'll have to really work at it. God deserves the very best you can do, doesn't he?"

Sara dug at the dirt with the toe of her shoe. "You're right, Mom," she said at last. "I don't want to waste the talent God gave me. I'd better go now and tackle that recital piece." Taking a seed with her, she added, "I'll glue this to my music, just to remind me."

TO DISCUSS

Do you have any talents? What are they? If you're not sure, what do you do best in your work or play? Could God use any of these in his service? Right now your talents and abilities are only possibilities. What can you do to make them realities? In the lessons on this theme, "Developing Christian Character," remember that you don't become perfect at once in any area of your Christian life. You must work hard at becoming the best you can be.

TO DO

On a piece of paper, list two or three things that you do best. Beside each one, write: (1) how I could use my talent to serve and honor God and (2) what I can do to improve my talent.

TO PRAY

Ask the Lord to help you find your best talents and to begin to work hard at developing them for him to use in whatever way he wants.

CHAPTER FORTY-SEVEN

Be Loving and Forgiving

Ephesians 4:29-32

Don't use bad language. Say only what is good and helpful to those you are talking to, and what will give them a blessing.

Don't cause the Holy Spirit sorrow by the way you live. Remember, he is the one who marks you to be present on that day when salvation from sin will be complete.

Stop being mean, bad-tempered, and angry. Quarreling, harsh words, and dislike of others should have no place in your lives. Instead, be kind to each other, tenderhearted, forgiving one another, just as God has forgiven you because you belong to Christ. TLB

Sara really wanted to win the ten dollar prize that would be given for the best costume in the Memorial Day parade. She lay awake one night, trying to decide what her costume should be. At last she had a brainstorm—she'd go as a giant box of candy. The next day she went to the grocery store and got a big, empty box. She carefully decorated it with red, white, and blue crepe paper and ribbons. When she got inside, it covered all but her feet. Two peepholes allowed her to see. There was a hinged door in front for throwing out candy to the judges.

On the parade day, Sara, in her box, joined other costumed children, ready to march. *How will Jodie be dressed?* she wondered. *She wouldn't tell me, even though I let her see my costume.*

"Hi! Is that you in there, Sara?"

Sara, recognizing Jodie's voice, slowly turned around to look through her peepholes. She almost bumped into—ANOTHER BOX! Jodie had a costume almost identical to her own. "I decided to surprise you so we could be the Boxy Twins," said Jodie. "Aren't we magnificent?"

Sara was furious! How dare Jodie copy her idea! But the parade was beginning, so they marched off together. They awkwardly bowed before the judges, tossing out candy. The judges laughed, and the audience cheered.

When the winner was announced, a judge said, "We all agreed that the boxes were the best, but there is only one first prize. So we are going to divide it between the two. Each will get five dollars." Sara forced a smile on her face, but she was fuming inside as she walked up and accepted the money. Not a word was said about whose idea the boxes had been.

"Mom, I'll never speak to Jodie again," declared Sara when she told her mother what had happened. "Can you believe what she did? Why should she share in the prize?"

"Easy, Honey," Mom said. "Jodie is a very good friend. Don't be so hasty." She gave Sara a big hug. "Think about Jesus, your best Friend, for a moment."

"What about him?" asked Sara. "He's not like Jodie. He's never done anything wrong to me."

"But you wronged him," said Mom, "and still he forgave all your sins and saved you. That's the way he wants us to treat others."

Sara was silent for a moment. "That's hard to do, Mom," she said finally. "But I know you're right. May I invite Jodie over for popcorn?"

TO DISCUSS

Is it easy to forgive someone who has wronged you? Which would you rather do—forgive, or get even? Which should be more important—keeping your friends, or having your own way? What did Jesus say on the cross about those who had put him there? Look at Ephesians 4:32. How are we supposed to forgive?

TO DO

Make a pretty friendship card from a sheet of construction paper. Fold it twice. Decorate the outside however you wish. Inside, print, "I thank God for a good friend like you." Give the card to the friend of your choice. If you have had a quarrel with that friend, wouldn't this be a good time to say, "I'm sorry"?

TO PRAY

Ask the Lord to help you forgive others, as he has forgiven you. If you have hard feelings against someone, go to him or her and make things right.

Be Honest in Word and Deed

Mike was saving money to buy a new bike. "I wish I could earn some money," he told Joshua. "But it's hard for a little kid to get a job."

"Hey, I know someone who might give you a job," said Joshua. "It's Mr. Hill. He's looking for a boy to help him do his yard work. He called and asked me if I could do it, but I said I couldn't because we'll be moving soon."

"Great!" exclaimed Mike. "I'll go talk to him now."

Mr. Hill was pleased to see Mike. "I've already told Max he could help me today," he said. "But I have extra things that need to be done right now, so I'll let both of you work. Then I'll decide on one of you who can help me one day each week."

Both boys worked hard all day, each trying to do

his best to please Mr. Hill. At the end of the day, Mr. Hill handed the boys their pay. "Here's ten dollars for each of you," he said, handing each of the boys one dollar bills.

On the way home, Mike happily counted his money. "Wait a minute," he said, stopping short. "If I counted right, there's too much money here." When he reached home, Mike carefully counted the money again. Sure enough, there was a dollar too much. His first thought was to keep the money. Mr. Hill would never know. But all through the evening, and even after he'd gone to bed, Mike was troubled. Since he knew that Mr. Hill had given him too much money, wouldn't keeping it be the same as stealing?

The next morning, very early, Mike knocked on Mr. Hill's door and told him, "You gave me a dollar too much. I thought last night that maybe I'd just keep it. But I couldn't do that. It's not honest."

Mr. Hill smiled and said, "I gave each of you boys too much money. It was a test. You see, the boy who works with me will be using my tools and sometimes going inside my house. I needed to know which boy I could trust. If Max doesn't return his dollar, the job is yours." A few days later, Mr. Hill called Mike to tell him he had the job.

When Mike told the Bible Explorers about the dollar, Mrs. Kendrick said,

"The Bible has a lot to say about honesty. It tells us that God hates lying. You can be dishonest both with your words and your actions. What are some ways in which a boy or girl might be dishonest?" The children named lying, stealing, cheating, not doing what you promise to do, gossiping (saying someone did something when you're not sure he or she did it), and not admitting it when you do wrong.

"It isn't always easy to be truthful," said Mrs. Kendrick, "especially if you know you may get punished if you admit you did wrong. But two wrongs never make a right. Someday God will hold you accountable for whether or not you have been honest. Also, just like in Mike's experience, people want to know whom they can trust. Start now to be honest in all things."

TO DISCUSS

Suppose you found a wallet with money in it and a name. No one saw you pick it up. What would be the honest thing to do? Suppose you and some friends are playing ball and accidentally break a window. The other children run away. What would you do? Suppose a friend asks you to tell his mother that he was with you when he wasn't. Would you help your friend to stay out of trouble by doing what he asks?

TO DO

Think carefully about your words and actions of the past. Is there something you have not been completely honest about? If so, tell the truth and make things right. Show God and all who know you that you are someone to be trusted.

TO PRAY

If you have been dishonest in any way, confess it to the Lord now and ask him to forgive you. Ask him to help you be honest, even though it's not always easy to do so.

CHAPTER FORTY-NINE

Be Joyful

TO READ

Matthew 5:10-12

Blessed are those who are persecuted because of righteousness, for theirs is the kingdom of heaven. Blessed are you when people insult you, persecute you and falsely say all kinds of evil against you because of me. Rejoice and be glad, because great is your reward in heaven, for in the same way they persecuted the prophets who were before you. NIV

Philippians 4:4

Rejoice in the Lord always. Again I will say, rejoice! NKJV

It sure is tough to do what's right in this neighborhood," complained Mike at a Bible Explorers meeting. "The other boys make fun of Josh and me because we try to obey Jesus."

"I know it's not easy on Christian kids these days," Mrs. Kendrick said sympathetically. "But Jesus tells us to rejoice when we are persecuted for his sake. Perhaps this true story about a little girl in Venezuela will help you:"

Joyful Cecilia

"Look at the big smile on Cecilia's face," Betty said to Paul. "I think she is the happiest child I've ever known." Missionaries Paul and Betty Alexander were standing outside a small church building in Venezuela, greeting the people as they arrived. "Since Cecilia asked Jesus to save her," Betty went on, "she seems to bubble over with happiness."

"Maria brings the little girl to church," Paul replied. "Perhaps she knows the reason for Cecilia's cheerfulness."

"Maria," Betty said later, "we can't help noticing how cheerful Cecilia is when she comes to church.

Is there a special reason why she is so filled with joy?"

Maria nodded her head. "Sí, I can tell you, Señora Betty," she said. "Church is the only place where Cecilia can find happiness. Did you know her mother and father are dead?"

"No, we didn't know," said Betty. "Where does she live?"

"Her only relative, an aunt, took her in. But she didn't want her," replied Maria. "She makes life miserable for the poor girl and treats her like a servant."

"Poor Cecilia has to work hard, then?" Betty asked.

"Sí, very hard," Maria said with a sigh. "Most mornings she has to be in the potato fields by four to hoe potatoes. Then she goes to school from seven until twelve. When she returns home, she has to clean the house and do other work. She even has to wash the clothes, scrubbing each piece by hand."

"I am amazed that she is as cheerful with such a hard life," said Betty. "I'll certainly give her all the attention and love I can."

One Sunday at church, Cecilia's bright smile was missing. "Is something wrong?" Betty asked her.

Cecilia nodded, her eyes wet with tears. "Oh, Señora Betty," she cried. "My aunt ripped up the Bible you gave me."

"I'm so sorry," said Betty. "Why did she destroy it?"

"She got mad because I took time to read it," Cecilia said. "She just wants me to work all the time." Suddenly a smile lit up her face. "At least she still lets me come to church," she added. "And she can't take Jesus away from me, can she? He keeps me happy inside, no matter what happens!"

As the story ended, Mike said, "I sure don't have as tough a time trying to do right as that little girl did. I'm going to ask Jesus to help me be happy always, just like her."

TO DISCUSS

Does anyone make fun of you for obeying Jesus? How do you react to this? What does Jesus want you to do when you are persecuted for his sake? (Find the answer in Matthew 5:10-12.) If you are happy inside, will others know it?

BECOMING LIKE JESUS

On a piece of paper, draw two identical faces, except for the mouths. Draw the first mouth with the corners of the mouth turned down in a frown. Draw the other mouth with the corners turned up in a smile. Underneath write, "If you have a little frown, turn it upside down. Jesus gives you joy."

Thank Jesus for his many blessings to you. Ask him to help you remember them when things go wrong. Trust him to make you joyful inside, no matter what happens.

CHAPTER FIFTY

Be Faithful

Revelation 2:10

Be faithful, even to the point of death, and I will give you the crown of life. NIV

"This is our last meeting of the Bible Explorers Club," Mrs. Kendrick said, looking a little sad. "Soon our family will be moving near the school where my husband and I will study before going to the mission field. All of you have been very faithful to attend our club meetings, you have really tried to learn God's Word, and you have grown spiritually. It's hard to find the words to tell you how much I appreciate you. Perhaps, though, these will give you some idea of how proud I am of you."

Mrs. Kendrick handed each child a beautifully printed certificate and a small gift. As they admired these, she said, "I know you have watched the Olympics on television. What do you suppose is the proudest moment for any of the athletes?"

"I think it's when they stand on the podium, wearing their gold medal and hearing their nation's anthem," said Mike. "If I were an athlete, that would be my proudest moment."

"Yeah, I'll bet then they are glad they trained so hard and kept working to be the best they could be," added Joshua.

"Only the athletes who have been faithfully keeping themselves in shape and who have practiced hard will ever go on to get the gold or other medals," said Mrs. Kendrick. "Today I gave you certificates for faithful work and attendance at Bible Explorers Club. But someday, if you continue to be faithful to the Lord, you will receive rewards that are far more important than these certificates or the Olympic gold medals.

"When you stand before Jesus at his judgment seat, he will examine your life," Mrs. Kendrick said. "He sees and knows everything you do, whether it is good or bad. At the judgment seat, Jesus will reward all the things you did to please him. In fact, the Bible says that the things you do for God are like gold, silver, and precious stones."

"Hey," said Mike, "maybe I'll get a gold medal in heaven!"

"That's right!" said Mrs. Kendrick. "If you don't remember all I have taught you, please never forget this: Be faithful to Jesus and 'go for the gold' in whatever you do. Now, Mike, will you close in prayer?"

"Dear Jesus," Mike prayed, "thank you for our wonderful teacher and for our Bible Explorers Club. Help us to remember what we've learned and to be faithful to you all our lives. Please take care of us all until we meet again. In Jesus' name, amen."

TO DISCUSS

What are some good works you can do for Jesus? Tell in your own words what being faithful to Jesus means to you.

TO DO

Solve the puzzle "What God Wants Me to Do Always." On a piece of paper, write a letter to Jesus. Thank him for all the ways that he loves you, and tell him some things you would like to do for him. Ask him to help you be faithful to him all your life.

TO PRAY

Ask the Lord to help you earn rewards in heaven someday—not for your glory, but for his.

What God Wants Me to Do Always

Print in the boxes, in order, the letter found in the first word, but not in the second. What does God want you to do?

1. In BRAKE . . . but not in RAKE

2. In CANE . . . but not in CAN

3. In LEFT . . . but not in LET

4. In SEAT . . . but not in SET

5. In PAIR . . . but not in PAR

6. In THE . . . but not in HE

7. In THEN . . . but not in TEN

8. In FLOW . . . but not in LOW

9. In DOUSE . . . but not in DOSE

10. In BLACK . . . but not in BACK

Answer is on page 232.

Answers to Quizzes

Answer to chapter 4 quiz

Who Hears Our Prayers?

1. Call upon the Lord every (A) D (Y). (Psalm 88:9)

   D   A   Y .

2. Search for God with all your   E   (R)   (A)   T   (H). (Jeremiah 29:13)

   H   E   A   R   T

3. Ask, and it shall be   (V)   I   (N)   (E)   G   to you. (Matthew 7:7)

   G   I   V   E   N

4. Have   (H)   A   (F)   I   (T). (Hebrews 11:6)

   F   A   I   T   H

5. When you pray,   (E)   B   (E)   V   I   E   (L). (Mark 11:24)

   B   E   L   I   E   V   E

WHO HEARS AND ANSWERS OUR PRAYERS?

Our   H   E   A   V   E   N   L   Y

   F   A   T   H   E   R

Answer to chapter 9 quiz

The Bible Said It Long Ago

He said that God sits on his throne ____above____ ____the____ ____circle____
____of____ ____the____ ____earth____

cat	man	circle	yellow	frog	laugh
dog	the	boy	blue	snake	earth
above	woman	girl	of	the	cry

Answer to chapter 13 quiz

What Does God Know?

1. *Psalm 147:4*   The names of all the _____ stars _____ .

2. *John 21:16*   If you _____ love _____ him.

3. *Acts 5:4*   If someone _____ lied _____ to him.

4. *Acts 15:8*   Your _____ heart _____ .

5. *Psalm 139:2*   Your _____ thought _____ .

6. *Matthew 10:30*   The number of _____ hairs _____ you have.

7. *Matthew 6:8*   What you _____ need _____ .

8. *Proverbs 15:3*   The wicked and the _____ good _____ .

9. *Psalm 139:3*   All your _____ ways _____ .

10.   John 16:30

#							
1.	s	t	a	r	s		
2.			l	o	v	e	
3.			l	i	e	d	
4.	h	e	a	r	t		
5.		t	h	o	u	g	h	t
6.		h	a	i	r	s	
7.			n	e	e	d	
8.			g	o	o	d	
9.		w	a	y	s		

Answer to chapter 19 quiz

Some Things to Remember about Jesus

1. He __showed__ us what God the Father is like (John 14:7).
2. He gave us an __example__ for living (1 Peter 2:21).
3. He never __sinned__ (1 Peter 2:22).
4. He came to destroy the works of the __devil__ (1 John 3:8).
5. He showed God's __love__ for the whole world (John 3:16).
6. He __taught__ God's truths. (Matthew 5:1-2).
7. He healed the __lepers__, the __blind__, the __deaf__, and the __lame__. He __raised__ the dead. He preached the __gospel__ (Matthew 11:5).
8. He __died__ for our sins and __rose__ again (1 Corinthians 15:3-4).
9. He went back to __heaven__ (Acts 1:9).

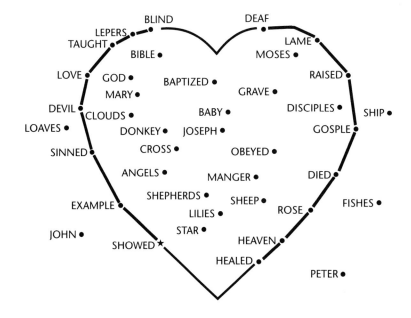

Answer to chapter 24 quiz

God Is in Charge of the Nations

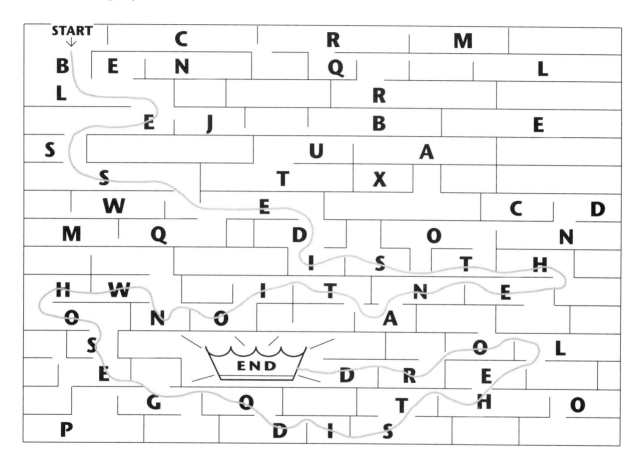

"B l e s s e d   i s   t h e   n a t i o n
w h o s e   G o d   i s   t h e   L o r d."

Psalm 33:12

Answer to chapter 27 quiz

God's Wonderful Angels

R S T U V W X Z

L M N P Q R S T

O P Q R S T V W

Q S T U V W X Y

A B C D E F H I

P Q R S T V W X

Y Z B C D E F G

K L M N O P Q S

C E F G H I J K

D E F G H J K L

T U V W X Y Z B

M O P Q R S T U

Z B C D E F G H

I J K L M O P Q

D E F H I J K L

A B C D F G H I

J K M N O P Q R

Y
O
U
R
■
G
U
A
R
D
I
A
N
■
A
N
G
E
L

A B C D E F G H I J K L M N O P Q R S T U V W X Y Z

Answer to chapter 30 quiz

1—D, 2—E, 3—A, 4—C, 5—B

Answer to chapter 32 quiz

The Results of Sin

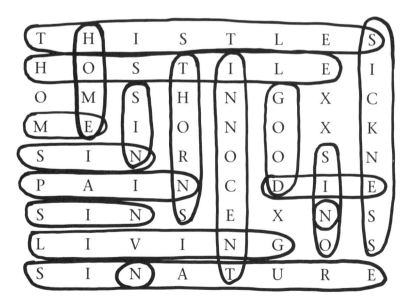

Answer to chapter 39 quiz

What Kind of Life Does Jesus Give?

What verse in the Bible do these words remind you of? <u>John 3:16</u>

If you $\underset{\text{C-1}}{\text{b}}$ $\underset{\text{D+1}}{\text{e}}$ $\underset{\text{J+2}}{\text{l}}$ $\underset{\text{L-3}}{\text{i}}$ $\underset{\text{C+2}}{\text{e}}$ $\underset{\text{U+1}}{\text{v}}$ $\underset{\text{F-1}}{\text{e}}$ in Jesus,

you will not $\underset{\text{O+1}}{\text{p}}$ $\underset{\text{G-2}}{\text{e}}$ $\underset{\text{T-2}}{\text{r}}$ $\underset{\text{F+3}}{\text{i}}$ $\underset{\text{T-1}}{\text{s}}$ $\underset{\text{F+2}}{\text{h}}$, but have

$\underset{\text{H-3}}{\text{e}}$ $\underset{\text{S+1}}{\text{t}}$ $\underset{\text{A+4}}{\text{e}}$ $\underset{\text{U-3}}{\text{r}}$ $\underset{\text{M+1}}{\text{n}}$ $\underset{\text{D-3}}{\text{a}}$ $\underset{\text{J+2}}{\text{l}}$

$\underset{\text{O-3}}{\text{l}}$ $\underset{\text{F+3}}{\text{i}}$ $\underset{\text{G-1}}{\text{f}}$ $\underset{\text{J-5}}{\text{e}}$

A B C D E F G H I J K L M N O P Q R S T U V W X Y Z

Answer to chapter 45 quiz

I Can Say No

I'm not a <u>chicken</u> or a <u>square</u>. I'm a Christian who has

<u>Jesus</u> in my <u>heart</u>. He is the <u>King</u> of kings.

If a <u>girl</u> or a <u>boy</u> asks me to do wrong, I will say NO

and proudly tell <u>everyone</u> that I <u>love</u> <u>Jesus</u>.

What God Wants Me to Do Always

1. In BRAKE . . . but not in RAKE

2. In CANE . . . but not in CAN

3. In LEFT . . . but not in LET

4. In SEAT . . . but not in SET

5. In PAIR . . . but not in PAR

6. In THE . . . but not in HE

7. In THEN . . . but not in TEN

8. In FLOW . . . but not in LOW

9. In DOUSE . . . but not in DOSE

10. In BLACK . . . but not in BACK

B
E
■
F
A
I
T
H
F
U
L